PLAYING FOR
THE RING

PLAYING FOR THE RING

THE GAME DON'T CHANGE
JUST THE PLAYERS

DR. ABDALLA RASHAD TAU

Independent Thinkers

PLAYING FOR THE RING

Copyright © 2017 by Dr. Abdalla Rashad Tau

Library of Congress Control Number: 2017905013

ISBN-13: 978-0-989318327
ISBN-10: 098931832X

Printed in USA by Independent Thinkers, Inc.

.

To Love, Family, & Happiness.

CONTENTS

WHY DR. TAU?

Why am I writing a relationship book? Why now? Why ever? Who am I? What makes me an authority on relationships? What is my angle? Why are men always writing relationship books for women? Why don't men write relationship books for men? These are the series of questions that others and even I have posed as I entertained the idea of writing a relationship book.

First and foremost, my reply is, "Why not me?" Giving full disclosure, I have never been married, I do not have any children, and I have never been in a long-term committed relationship. However, I have had my share of relationships, interactions, and conversations with the female *Species*, and let's just say, I have learned a lot about what to do and what not to do, if and when I encounter "The One." Now, would I classify myself as an authority on the topic? Absolutely not. But, I do have a voice.

For women that often pose the question, "Why are men always writing relationship books geared toward women?" The short answer is that men are not seeking to read these types of books. However, I believe they should, because men can benefit a great deal from this body of work and similar literature.

I have heard countless stories about what's wrong with men and what they need to do, as well as with women and what they need to do. Some things I agreed with, other things I did not. I have also been a member of several relationship panels on the radio and at various live events. Not to mention the countless relationship parties where men and women, mostly single, continuously joust with each other about whose right or wrong and what they NEED to and SHOULD do to satisfy the other. I find these modalities to be redundant and counterproductive.

Yes, we speak two different languages: men speak penis and women speak vagina, but under the right circumstances we go so well together. Men and women both contribute to the success and/or demise of relationships equally. Instead of constantly testing and battling each other, concentrating on how much we differ, our time could be utilized more efficiently if we focused more on our similarities.

Look, I get it, "Men are from Mars and Women are from Venus," but that doesn't mean we can't amicably cohabitate in the same solar system, figuratively speaking. If we don't learn more harmonious ways of interacting, relationships will continue to diminish, homes will continue to be broken, and more children will grow up in single parent households. Playing For The Ring is a collection of research, observations, scenarios, and experiences and my solution to this conundrum. Furthermore, it is my contribution to the ongoing conversation related to creating healthier relationships, raw and uncensored.

PLAYING FOR
THE RING

Osram Ne Nsoromma

"The Moon and the Star"

Symbol of Love, Faithfulness, Harmony

"Osram Ne Nsoromma reflects the

harmony that exists in the bonding

between a man and woman."

INTRODUCTION

RING

Have you ever paid attention to what many professional athletes say in interviews when asked, "Why do you play the game?" "Why are you leaving your team to play with another franchise?" or "What is your overall goal?" Beyond the money, materialism, and women, the answer is often, "a title" or "a championship *Ring*." In the realms of the professional sports world, specifically Major League Baseball (MLB), the National Football League (NFL), and the National Basketball Association (NBA), most athletes have one major goal in mind – to win a championship *Ring*. They want that title. Yes, of course they love making the money, living in big houses, driving expensive cars, sleeping with groupies, and the adulation from adoring fans; however, all the aforementioned benefits of being a professional athlete pale in comparison with being able to forever say - "I am a champion." or "I have a championship *Ring.*"

There are many great athletes that have had very successful careers. Athletes such as Charles Barkley, Barry Bonds, Randy Moss, and Jim Kelly, made an abundance of money, hold sports records that may never be broken, and have even played in championship games, yet that sought-after *Ring* has eluded them. Unfortunately, after they have retired from the game ringless, it becomes a stigma that is attached to their legacy. They are reminded constantly that even though they had a great career, they never acquired a *Ring*.

"What does perfection look like to me? Championship Rings."
- Kobe Bryant

In many ways, I see a parallel between professional athletes and women with regard to how they function in relationships. They are both <u>Playing For The Ring</u>. Also, just like the athlete, it doesn't matter how successful she is, it doesn't matter if she attains the highest degrees in the land, makes billions of dollars, starts countless businesses, or even becomes one of the most well-known people on the planet. If she does not bag a husband and have children, she will always have the proverbial asterisk by her name because she is ringless, as far as some people are concerned, that is. Nevertheless, the quest for the *Ring* begins at a very early age due to her social and environmental conditioning.

RING

This dogma begins during the adolescent years and is influenced through socialization. Anthropologists, politicians, sociologists, educationalists, and social psychologists use the term socialization to describe the process of how individuals adopt various philosophies, norms, and customs of the social order they exist in. Socialization is learned through five major agents: Family, Education, Community, Peer Groups, and Mass Media.

The initial and most important agent of socialization is family, more specifically one's parents. Parents are the greatest influence in a child's social development. Another important phase of socialization derives from education or school. School is where children interact with others and are introduced to a formal and informal curriculum. Both help to shape their beliefs and values. Community and culture expose individuals to religious views and cultural traditions. Peer groups influence thought processes, dress code, tastes in music, and other aspects of life. On one hand friends offer support and companionship, but the downside may be a source of negative peer pressure. Finally, there is mass media, which socializes people through the internet, movies, television, magazines, music, and books. These agents of socialization influence fashion trends, political views, culture, and various other practices and beliefs. The

entire concept of <u>Playing For The Ring</u> is a byproduct of socialization.

> *"If a man cannot buy me a diamond Ring, we cannot get married."*
> *- Xena*

Still not a believer? Not a problem. Let's explore a scenario you may have personally experienced, or you may have possibly seen play out with your peers, on social media, on television, or in movies. Whenever a woman becomes engaged and congregates with her girlfriends and/or female family members and says, "Guess what, I'm engaged." or "He popped the question." What is the first thing her girlfriends ask her? It never fails. They say, "Let me see the *Ring*." They are extremely excited for their friend and her *Ring*. Anything related to the husband-to-be seems irrelevant and is rarely discussed at that moment. All they want to know about is the *Ring*. How big is the *Ring*? How many karats is the *Ring*? How much did the *Ring* cost? Have you had the *Ring* appraised yet? All the emphasis is put on the *Ring* and of course the wedding; not on the man that she supposedly wants to be with for eternity and procreate with, or the *Marriage* itself. One would have to ask, does this make sense?

RING

"I want a diamond Ring so I can show it off. I know it may seem superficial and I've been brainwashed to desire it, but I don't care. I want it anyway."
- Katlyn

Unfortunately, many women have been led to believe that an expensive wedding *Ring*, a diamond wedding *Ring* in particular, is an indication of how much a man loves her. Ladies, I'm here to tell you, IT IS NOT. If it did, all women with diamond wedding *Rings* would have very successful unions, and we all know that is not the case. Don't fret, it's not your fault ladies. You have been conditioned from a very young age to not just believe that you had to have a *Ring* to get married, but you had to have a certain type of *Ring* in order to be married. The information you are about to absorb from the pages of <u>Playing For The Ring</u> can be utilized in a proactive, active, or unfortunately, in a reactive fashion depending on the age (teens, young adult, middle age) and station (married, divorced, separated, parent) of the person. The requirement of a diamond *Ring* is typically the most prominent staple females are wishing for prior to the *Fairytale* wedding. Have you ever pondered the origins of this indoctrination?

✸ PLAYING FOR THE RING

HISTORICAL VIEW

MYTHICAL VALUE

Essentially, the entire *Fairytale* concept is predicated on the *Ring*: Diamond *Rings* in particular. These *Rings* are considered to be precious and priceless. Ironically, they are not. "Why?" you ask. Because diamonds are actually worthless! Let me say it one more time, "Diamonds are worthless!" They are no different than any rock you may unearth, except that they are really shiny and many people find beauty in their appearance.

Diamonds are unjustifiably expensive because, contrary to what people have been led to believe, they are not actually scarce. In fact, if used for industrial purposes they would only be worth between $2 to $30, contingent on the weight of the stone. The illusion is created by big diamond companies purposefully controlling the supply and fabricating artificial scarcity, which has led to exorbitant prices for rocks that have no real value. The value is mythical. Additionally, the diamond industry amongst others, has some very unethical practices, specifically on the continent of Africa. Let's touch on the unethical practices in Africa first.

> *"I have personally never and will never purchase diamonds for anyone, unless certain things about the diamond industry changes."*
> *- Kinte'*

Until the 19th century, India and Brazil were the only known diamond producing countries. Diamonds were so scarce that even various monarchs and noblemen found it very challenging to acquire the stones. The concept of the general public having access to diamonds was absurd until 1867 when diamonds were first excavated in South Africa. Even though the supply of diamonds increased rapidly, which would suggest lower prices, the idea of diamonds as a rare and precious commodity was sustained, by design.

A great majority of the diamonds in the world come from African countries. However, much of the diamond industry is controlled by Western corporations, namely De Beers, a South African based diamond company that dominates much of the international diamond industry. The citizens of African countries such as South Africa, Angola, Sierra Leone, and Botswana only see a small fraction of the profits generated from their diamond mines, if that. Additionally, the citizens of these African nations experience adverse situations and realities (e.g., intentional European underdevelopment, poverty, abuse, and death) because of the diamond industry's unfair and sinister business practices.

De Beers is a diamond company founded by Cecil Rhodes in the late 19th century. Cecil Rhodes was a British terrorist, colonist, and imperialist in South Africa who formed the British South African Company (BSAC), which colonized Zimbabwe and acquired a British Royal Charter. He was a Member of Parliament in the Cape Colony and was also Prime Minister of the Cape Colony.

Between 1874 and 1875 Rhodes along with his partner, Charles D. Rudd, consolidated a number of diamond mines and purchased the diamond rich farm named De Beers, also known as the Vooruitzicht Farm. The farm was named after the De Beers brothers, Diederik Arnoldus and Johannes Nicolaas, the original owners. This farm is where the name of Cecil Rhodes' diamond empire derived.

Over the next few years, utilizing his shrewd business tactics, Rhodes ultimately managed to acquire control of most of the world's diamond cartel, making him a very wealthy man who dominated the diamond industry. By 1887, De Beers was the sole owner of all the diamond mines in South Africa. Concurrently, Rhodes acquired complete control of the distribution channels through "The Diamond Syndicate," a conglomerate of merchants in Kimberley, South Africa who agreed to his terms of business. The syndicate understood that both parties' interests were compatible, which was the goal of scarcity coupled with high prices. Ultimately, Rhodes created a system that influenced prices in the diamond market that were undisturbed for nearly a century.

As time went on, the company continued to grow with various prominent influences. In 1926, after major opposition from board members, a German immigrant named Ernest Oppenheimer gained ownership and full control of De Beers. In 1927, De Beers was further financed by investors, The Rothschild Group and Alfred Beit. The Rothschild Group was a British multinational investment company owned by the Rothschild Family. Alfred Beit was a British South African that was a diamond and gold tycoon. De Beers dominated all areas of the diamond industry including mining, industrial manufacturing, and trading. Rhodes and his company De Beers single-handedly revolutionized and monopolized the diamond industry by converting rocks with no real value into symbols of glamour, romance, and prestige.

"I contend that we are the first race in the world, and that the more of the world we inhabit the better it is for the human race. Just fancy those parts that are at present inhabited

by the most despicable specimen of human beings, what an alteration there would be in them if they were brought under Anglo-Saxon influence...if there be a God, I think that what he would like me to do is paint as much of the map of Africa British Red as possible..."
- Cecil John Rhodes

In order to fabricate and maintain the high price tag on diamonds, De Beers created a high demand by stockpiling diamonds and only releasing a certain quantity per year. Additionally, they orchestrated a campaign claiming that diamonds were a symbol of love and commitment. In 1947, this campaign was furthered by De Beers using a psychological approach. This is the year when the phrase "A Diamond is Forever" was coined by N. W. Ayer and Son, an advertising company that utilized the phrase in De Beer's marketing campaigns.

The objective of the campaign was to make the diamond engagement *Ring* a psychological necessity as it relates to *Marriage*. Their target audience was 70 million people, ages 15 and over whose opinion they were seeking to influence. N. W. Ayer devised a very clever plan to arrange lectures to be facilitated at high schools across the nation. The purpose of those lectures was to indoctrinate young, impressionable females with the concept of a diamond engagement *Ring* as being a compulsory part of the *Marriage* process. De Beers spent millions of dollars deceiving the public into thinking they needed to purchase a product with *Mythical Value* on certain holidays, for special occasions, and particularly for *Marriage*.

> *"A gemstone is the ultimate luxury product. It has no material use. Men and women desire to have diamonds not for what they [diamonds] can do but for what they desire."*
> *- Nickey Oppenheimer, De Beers Deputy Chairman*

In the 21st century, the *Mythical Value* of diamonds is further propagated through movies, music, celebrities, social media, and advertisements with slogans such as, "Diamonds are a girl's best friend." "Every kiss begins with Kay." and "He went to Jared!" Ironically, the fervor for these symbols of love continues to grow despite the increasing number of individuals opting for divorce in America.

> *"If you liked it then you should have put a Ring on it."*
> *- Beyoncé Knowles – Carter, Single Ladies*

Obviously, the size or value of the *Ring* has no bearing on the success or lack thereof of a *Marriage*. In essence, being presented with a diamond *Ring* for *Marriage* is a false guarantee of success, especially if there is no substance behind the rock. I know what you are thinking, "So what's the alternative?" My answer is to be creative and original. Do something that is unique to your union. Make it special. Don't put all the emphasis on the *Ring*.

"I could care less about a freaking Ring. Most of my girlfriends had huge luxurious weddings, wore extravagant wedding dresses, took beautiful expensive pictures, and yes, received the coveted diamond Ring. Now they're all divorced. Can you live in a Ring? Can you drive a Ring? Can you cuddle with a Ring? I'm almost 40. I just want a good man. I'm over it."

~ Janet

☽ PLAYING FOR THE RING

CANDY CANE

WISH LIST

Whether people want to admit it or not, everybody has expectations of others. By definition the word expectation means a strong belief that something will happen in the future. The word is synonymous with hope. In relationships, people of both sexes expect or hope to have a certain type of companion. Depending on how they define a relationship, their expectations will embody certain ideologies and qualities that mirror their own. Often, people have a specific list of things they are seeking in a significant other. Thus, their ultimate goal is to hitch their wagon to an individual that embodies the philosophies and qualities on their list.

"A goal without a plan is just a wish."
- Herman Edwards

Proper planning is essential to achieving any goal. For instance, before a person goes grocery shopping, they may

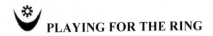

prepare a list to avoid purchasing unnecessary items. When determining the logistics of a family vacation, one may compile a list of places to travel, various hotels for lodging, and compare prices to prevent unforeseen issues while away from home. As with the aforementioned examples, people also have a list of characteristics and requirements for potential mates. Women in particular have a very specific set of qualifications when it comes to a potential suitor. Don't get me wrong, men do as well, but women seem to have a more extensive list. The question is, do you possess the same qualities that you admire and desire? And if you don't, do you at least possess the qualities that will complement the individual you're seeking? This is important, because if not, your list may remain just a wish.

> *"What are you bringing to the table? You can't just show up with an appetite thinking you're going to eat if all you have is a bowl and chop sticks."*
>
> *-Lee*

From my experience, I have found that people from their early teens and older have a list of what they are looking for in the opposite sex or significant other, whether they are cognizant of it or not. Some people may have a physical list, others simply date the same type of person habitually, which indicates that there is a certain type of person they're attracted to, which may

basically constitute a list. However, this list may vary by age and circumstance. Circumstances consist of, but are not limited to, the presence or absence of children and marital status. Your personal filters (education level, ethnicity) may also fluctuate. Through primary research such as surveys, focus groups, and observations, I have compiled information from males and females that range in age from 14 to 48, discussing specifically what they are looking for in a potential mate.

The data is featured in eight tables representing four different age groups (teens, 20s, 30s, 40s), with five lists of responses per table. I chose this age range because statistically it is the period when most people procreate and get married. It also represents a woman's most fertile years. I conducted focus groups and individual interviews with approximately 200 male and female participants. My request was for them to give me a list of everything they were looking for in a companion. I also asked six questions:

1. How old are you?
2. What is your marital status?
3. How many children do you have?
4. Do you want to get married?
5. Do you want a big wedding?
6. Do you want to buy (male)/receive (female) a diamond *Ring*?

Pay attention to the similarities, differences, and changes as the ages and life circumstances of the participants evolve.

Potential Man List A				
Respondent 1				
Strong Minded		Taller Than Me		Open-Minded
Trustworthy	Wants To Travel		Family Man	Protector
Ambition	Faithful	Handsome	Generous	Spoils Me
Respondent 2				
Protector		Father Figure		Supportive
Spoils Me	Taller Than Me		Good Job	Similar Beliefs
Not Abusive		Clean		Nice Body
Respondent 3				
Smart	Independent	Attractive	Loving	Caring
Strong	Funny	Groomed	Mature	Respectful
Respondent 4				
Intelligent		Kind		Funny
Pretty Teeth	Understanding		Soft Lips	Protective
Healthy		Mature		Supportive
Respondent 5				
Loyalty		Optimistic		Loving
Hardworking	Adventurous		Romantic	Communicator
Smart		Humble		Honesty

(Teenage Females, 0 Children)

Themes: The recurring themes amongst the teenage females were wanting a guy that possessed strength or protection, taller than them, generous or kind, supportive/caring, and intelligent.

Circumstances: The circumstances of these teenage females consisted of living with parents that were responsible for their well-being, going to school daily, dealing with the transition from childhood to womanhood (puberty), trying to fit in with a particular social group, peer pressure, and trying to figure out

what they were going to do after graduating from high school, amongst other things. Additionally, none of these young ladies had experienced *Marriage*, divorce, or having children.

Potential Woman List A-1			
Respondent 1			
Sexy	Classy	Can Cook	Long Hair
Big Booty	Smart	Funny	Independent
Nice Breasts	Belief In God	Good Attitude	Flat Stomach
Respondent 2			
Own Style		Decent Booty	
Pretty	Unique	Nice Smile	Decent Titties
Good Personality		Goal Oriented	
Respondent 3			
Big Butt	Athletic Body		Not Goofy
Little Make-Up & Weave		Can Sing & Dance	
Cute	Short	Long Hair	Classy
Respondent 4			
Confidence	Trustworthy	Good Looks	Athletic
Open To New Things	Likes To Explore		Good Personality
Fun	Smiles A Lot	Funny	Loves Music
Respondent 5			
Beautiful	Funny	Helpful	Intelligent	Successful
Independent		Acts Like A Lady	Understanding	
Stylish	Trustworthy	Unique	Focused	Strong

(Teenage Males, 0 Children)

Themes: The themes for these teenage males seemed related more to the physicality of their female counterpart. Themes encompassed long hair, good looks/beauty, nice breasts, and big booties.

Circumstances: Circumstances for these young men were similar to the young ladies as far as being cared for by their parents, attending school, puberty, peer pressure, and trying to

fit in. Additionally, these males were trying to figure out what it took to be a man. Similar to the teenage females, *Marriage*, divorce, and children were not yet a factor.

Potential Man List B				
Respondent 1				
Sharp Dresser		Ambitious		Smart Working
Supportive	Good Income		God-Fearing	Compassionate
Nice Car	Kind	Respectful	Moldable	Intelligent
Respondent 2				
Intellectual	Humble	Faithful	Career	Attractive
Adventurous	Mild-Tempered		Owns House	Good Sex
Humor	Personality	No Kids	Romantic	Traveler
Respondent 3				
Nice Fingers		Go Getter		Nice Teeth
NO Kids		God-Fearing		Athletic Build
Treats Me Like A Queen		A Lot Taller Than Me		Goal Oriented
Intellectual		Adventurous		Provider
Nice Smooth Chocolate Skin			Doing Equal Or Better Than Me	
Respondent 4				
Loving		Respectful	Caring	Fun
God-Fearing		Family Oriented		Understanding
Respondent 5				
Honest		Funny	Great Sex	Loyalty
Open-Minded		Adventurous		Team Player

(Females in their 20s, 0 Children)

Themes: Similar to females in their teens, these women in their 20s felt intelligence was an important quality for men to have. Other themes emerged such as wanting a man that is God-fearing, and good in bed.

Circumstances: These women had recently graduated from college, were starting their careers, and enjoying the single life. *Marriage*, divorce, and children were not a factor yet.

Potential Woman List B-1			
Respondent 1			
Great Caregiver	High Sexual Appetite		Unconditional Loyalty
Educated	Ambitious	Considerate	Spontaneous
Good Looks	Slim & Curvy		Can Cook
Respondent 2			
Intelligent	Goal Oriented		Attractive
Respondent 3			
Makes Me Laugh	God-Fearing	Natural Looks	No Weave
A Little Pudge Okay	Track Star Body		Family Oriented
Booty	Balanced		Fighter
No Make-Up	In Shape	Understanding	Adaptable
Respondent 4			
Communicator	Willing To Grow		No Attitude
Intelligent	Easy Going Personality		Pretty Smile
Respondent 5			
Traits Of A Good Mother		Try To Be A Good Cook	
Good Sense Of Humor	Have Class		Freak In The Bedroom
Submissive	Smart	Beautiful	Caring

(Males in their 20s, 0 Children)

Themes: While the physical aspects of a woman remained important to men in their 20s, intelligence emerged as equally important, along with being able to cook, and being good in bed.

Circumstances: The males were also starting their careers, graduating from college and enjoying the single life. *Marriage,* divorce, and children were not a factor.

> *"Why in the world would I get married now? It's too much pussy out here to just be married to one woman. If I got married now, I would definitely cheat on her."*
> *- Preston*

Potential Man List C				
Respondent 1				
Well Groomed		Financially Responsible	Family Oriented	
Christian	Selfless	Educated	Leader	Travels
Shared Values		God-Fearing	Enjoy Life	
Open-Mind	Ambitious	Attractive	Perseverance	Trustworthy
*Respondent 2				
Spiritual Connection With Jesus			Fiscal Responsibility	
Confidence		Vulnerability	Intelligence	
Have A Plan			Have A Mentor	
Respondent 3				
Honesty	Healthy	Ambitious	Loyal	Spiritual
Good Communicator			Sense Of Humor	
Attractive		Good Finances	Faithful	
Respondent 4				
Spiritual Relationship With God			Cool Under Pressure	
Confident		Loves Family	Leader	
Listens		Flexible	Best Friend	
Fitness & Sound Diet		Sexually Attentive	Exposure To Life	
Validates Me		Financially Responsible	Mature	
*(2) Respondent 5				
Gainfully Employed		Prayer A Daily Routine	Likes Cuddling	
Treats My Girls As Their Own		Engaged In The Granularity Of Life		
Enjoys A Splurge Occasionally		Involved In The Community		
God-Fearing		Family Oriented		
Likes Sports & Travel		Encouraging	Life Partner	

(Females in their 30s, (1, 2, 3...) Children, *Divorced)

Themes: Religion was a major factor for these women in their 30s, specifically a belief in Christianity and Jesus. Other themes included, financial responsibility, and being family oriented.

Circumstances: There were significant differences with these women in their 30s compared to the young ladies in their 20s. Two of the five women had experienced *Marriage* and divorce. The other women had a desire to be married, and were ready to

8

start a family. One woman was a single mother of two young girls as a result of her divorce and she had full custody.

Potential Woman List C-1			
Respondent 1			
Go Getter	Nice Ass	Team Player	Pretty Face
Good Personality	God-Fearing		People Person
Respondent 2			
Smart	Funny	Cute	Nice Booty
Natural Hair	Knows God		Pretty Face
Lips	Truthful	Sings	Thick
***(1) Respondent 3**			
Best Friend	Easy Going		No Yelling
Doesn't Complain	Respects Me As A Man		Doesn't Withhold Sex
Gets Along With Family & Daughter		Does Things to Make Me Happy	
Knows How To Communicate		We Have A Good Time Together	
Cool	Go To Church		Can Cook
Respondent 4			
Uninhibited	Spiritual Not Religious		Natural
Loyal	Classy	Healthy	Ambitious
Intelligent	Conscious	No Kids	Independent
Athletic Body	Non-Complacent	African Origin	Adventurous
Respondent 5			
Tall	Driven	Slim	Funny	Educated
Politically/Socially Aware		Militant		

(Males in their 30s, (1, 2, 3...) Children, *Divorced)

Themes: The themes for men in their 30s were somewhat similar to men in their 20s. Once again, a nice booty, pretty face, athletic body, and intelligence were similar themes. Additionally, religion or spirituality was an emerging theme for men in their 30s.

Circumstances: Men in their 30s were still progressing in their careers. *Marriage* was not necessarily at the forefront of their

9

mind. Only one of the respondents had experienced *Marriage* and divorce. Respondent 3 had one female child from his *Marriage*. The mother had full custody of their child.

Potential Man List D				
(1) Respondent 1				
Trained In A Field/College Educated		Believes Christ Is The Son Of God		
No Small Children		Happy In Career		
High School Graduate		Attends Church Regularly		
Saved	Cooks/Clean	Handy Man		Provider
***(2) Respondent 2**				
Loyal	Faithful	In Shape	Good Penis	Intelligent
No Small Kids		Attractive	Non-Judgmental	
Freaky	Ambitious	Compassionate		Funny
(1) Respondent 3				
Caring	Patient		Clean	Provider
Loves God	A Man of His Word		Good Sex	
Actions Speak For Himself		No Baby Mama Drama		
Responsible	Supportive		Honest	Hardworking
***(2) Respondent 4**				
Sense Of Humor		A Provider	Gainfully Employed	
Communicates	Intelligent	Integrity		Balanced
Christian	Loyal	Confident	Caring	Respectful
Initiative	Attractive	Ambitious	Faithful	Independent
***(1) Respondent 5**				
Great Sense Of Humor		No Young Children		
Attractive To Me	Family Ties		Sexual Appetite	
45 Or Older	Enterprising		Monogamous	
Spiritual	Charismatic	Leader		Loving

(Females in their 40s, (1, 2, 3...) Children, *Divorced)

Themes: Themes for females in their 40s consisted of not wanting a man with small children, a provider, good sex, believes in God/goes to church, and loyalty.

Circumstances: Significant differences from the 30s to 40s have taken place. Three of the five women had experienced

Marriage and divorce. All five women had procreated at least once and their children were older and in some cases out of the house. The children that had not left home lived with their mothers.

Potential Woman List D-1				
*(1) Respondent 1				
Love	Humility	Compassionate	Intelligent	Supportive
Affectionate	Caring	Domesticated	Trustworthy	Loyal
*(1) Respondent 2				
Responsible		Well Educated		Neat
Good Health		Versatile		Open-Minded
*(3) Respondent 3				
Fine	Ambitious	Spiritual	Beautiful	Loving
Sexually In Tuned		Intelligent		Financially Endowed
(3) Respondent 4				
Loyalty	Honesty	Virtuous	Devoted	Dependable
Awesome Personality		Believe In Higher Power		Bedroom Skills
(1) Respondent 5				
Respect	Affectionate	Great in Bed	Team Player	Responsible
Believe In The Most High		Maintain Her Appearance		

(Males in their 40s, (1, 2, 3...) Children, *Divorced)

Themes: The themes for men in their 40s were simple. They consisted of wanting a woman with intelligence, a nice body, good sex, and a belief in a higher power.

Circumstances: Men in their 40s also experienced significant differences compared to men in their 30s. Three of the five male respondents had experienced *Marriage* and divorce. All five men had procreated at least once. The major difference compared to their 40-year-old female counterparts was that they didn't have custody of their children.

Remember, these lists are merely examples of what males and females look for in the opposite sex at different stages of their lives under varied circumstances. The outcomes of this exercise may differ, contingent upon different variables related to ethnicity, belief systems, social economic status, and levels of education. Compile your own list of what you are looking for in the opposite sex and see how it stacks up with individuals in your social circle and potential mates. Another variable to consider is that women generally have one list, which is a barometer of the type of men they may consider having a long-term relationship with, and ultimately marrying. If a certain gentleman does not make the cut, he tends to fall into the friend zone or is completely dismissed. Some men, on the other hand, may have two lists, a *Marriage* material list and a recreation list.

Recreation

The recreation list is rarely ever discussed. Sadly, the only thing a woman needs to qualify for this list is to possess a heartbeat and a vagina! So, let's dig in: Men have two main categories in which women are assigned: *Marriage* material and recreation. There may be various sub lists under these main lists contingent on the man and his situation. It's more of an unspoken list that's not discussed, yet applied more often than not. Once you are assigned to the recreation category, it's very

difficult, almost impossible, to escape. The aforementioned lists given by the males are designated for women that are deemed *Marriage* material. The lists for recreation are not that extensive because expectations are minimal. You're probably asking, "Am I recreation?" "Have I ever been recreation?" or "How do I know if I'm recreation or *Marriage* material?" Here are a few indicators that you may be recreation:

- If you never see him in natural sunlight.
- If you never meet his friends or family members.
- If he doesn't mind sharing you sexually with others.
- If you don't see or hear from him the entire time you are on "injured reserve" (menstrual cycle).

Her: "Hey, I just received your voicemail message. I'm on my cycle, but I can still come over."

Him: "Mmmm... that's okay, I just remembered, I have something to do."

- If he never kisses you in the mouth.
- If he is okay with receiving oral sex, but refuses to return the favor.
- If you cannot call him and discuss personal issues.
- If he never takes you on a date.
- If he is ready for you to leave his house as soon as you finish having sex.

"As long as you have women that are complacent, accept mediocrity, and have low self-esteem, the concept of recreation will persist."
- Jerome

If you have experienced any or all of the aforementioned situations, you may be recreation. Ultimately you determine your fate (*Marriage* material or recreation) by your actions. In addition to these indicators, women have indirect and direct tests they administer to gauge whether or not, or how much a man cares about them - to see where his mind is as it relates to her. This is essentially a way to see if they are in fact recreation or *Marriage* material. I've coined these tests Vagina Tests. Hold on! Hold on! Before you get upset about me using the phrase Vagina Tests, let me inform you that men also perform similar tests, called Penis Tests.

However, Penis Tests have a completely different purpose. Penis Tests basically measure if, when, and how a man is going to have sex with a woman. Yes, Penis Tests are only about sex, nothing else. Again, both Vagina Tests and Penis Tests can be barometers for whether a person is recreation or *Marriage* material. Let's look at some examples that may vary from person to person. The ins and outs of recreation will be discussed further in a later chapter.

Vagina Test

I have a 90-day rule. I don't have sex with men for the first 90 days. Are you okay with that?
Did you think about me today?
My cycle is still on, but do you feel like coming over so we can cuddle and watch movies?
What are the characteristics of your ideal wife?
Do you mind if I leave some clothes over here, so I don't have to pack a bag when I spend the night?
Would you be upset if I had sex with someone else?

"The 90-day rule is the quintessential Vagina Test. That is the worst test to give a man. You have basically given him a date for when he's going to get the booty. He is simply going to wait you out, but while he's waiting, he will have sex with other women on the side. Duhhh!!!"
- Johnny

Penis Test

You look a little tense. Would you like a massage?
What type of panties are you wearing?
When was your last menstrual cycle? How many days does your menstrual cycle last? Is this your last day?
Are you going home to freshen up before you come see me?
Instead of going out to eat, may I cook for you?
What's the freakiest thing you've done sexually?

"Don't wait until after you give up the booty and then ask to be taken on a date. It's too late. Dinners, movies, flowers, & concerts are merely vehicles to get to the booty."
- Ricky

As you're making your list applicable to real life situations and relationships, continue to keep in mind that you will most likely not get everything you're looking for. Is it possible? It depends on who you ask. Your most important task is to differentiate between what you really need versus what you really want. Additionally, determine what your "deal breakers" are. Deal breakers are aspects of an individual that will absolutely disqualify them from any consideration as a mate. Examples of deal breakers could be fundamental differences in religious beliefs, drug use, having children, smoking cigarettes, or financial illiteracy.

"So, you think it's unfair that well-put-together men always want women to change to meet their high expectations and specificities. Yet, those are the only men you seek. I'm sure there are about three or four guys pursuing you right now, who will take you exactly as you are. Why don't you give them a chance? They don't want you to change? Oh, that's right, you are not interested in them."
- Denzel

Fishing

You're possibly saying: "I have my list and I'm already applying all these techniques in my dating process, yet I continuously produce the same results, running into the same wrong person." Additionally asking: "What am I doing wrong?" "Why can't I find what I'm looking for on my list?" "Can't I just cast out a net and hope I catch what I'm seeking?" The answer may be two-fold. The problem is either the "bait" you're using or the "body of water" where you are fishing. By examining those two areas, you may realize you have to change one or both. For example, if you wish to catch swordfish and you're fishing in a pond using crickets as bait, you will never accomplish your goal. You are using the wrong bait and fishing in the wrong body of water, yet you're wondering why you keep catching catfish. Let's apply this concept to real life situations.

"Well, that's where you messed up son you can't go to no bar to find a nice woman. You gotta go to a nice place, a quiet place like a library, there's good women there and 'erm, church, they're good girls. Oh oh, where I'm going tonight, to the Black Awareness Rally, it's gone be nice clean girls. That's where I'm going, shit...."
- Clarence, Coming to America

First, let's clearly outline bait and bodies of water. The type of bait you are utilizing can be a number of things. Your initial bait is your appearance. As you can see with the male's *Wish List*, men are physical beings. When you get dressed in the morning, ask yourself what your appearance is saying before you walk out of the house. Pay attention to how you wear your hair, apply your make-up, or the type of clothes you wear and how you wear them. Are you deliberately trying to send a message or are you oblivious? Are you saying: "Hey I am easy, just buy me a 2-piece chicken and biscuit meal and you can get the booty?" Or are you saying: "Hello, I'm a woman and I will be treated with respect at all times?" How you present yourself could send either message.

Additionally, your bait could consist of your quality of intellect and conversation. For example, are you a sapiosexual who requires mental stimulation at all times or are you satisfied with simply discussing sports and the weather? Knowing what type of interactions you prefer will better help determine who and what complements you.

Bodies of water simply refer to where you are meeting certain types of men. Are you meeting men at bars, the gas station, a library, or the grocery store? Yes, it matters. You have to be very deliberate in your movements. Along with your list, outline your objectives and then you can decide where to find

exactly what you're looking for. For instance, if one of the major objectives on your list is to have someone that cares about their health and fitness, where would you find him? Would he be shopping at the famers market for fresh fruits and vegetables or devouring hot wings and drinking alcohol at the local watering hole? If you desire someone that is highly intellectual, would this person most likely be attending a conference that features orators discussing world politics or "making it rain" at the strip club? Also, are you presenting yourself as a person that is representative of the former or latter examples? Recognize that they go hand in hand.

"I was like this when you met me. Why are you trying to change me now?"
- Connie

Again, no matter what your list consists of, you are probably not going to get everything you want in or from one person. However, you can get the majority of what you want and learn to accept the small things you don't like. Don't worry, your counterpart will probably have to make identical concessions. You must also consider that people may change over time. With needs, wants, and expectations changing over time, your list of wants, or the attributes you possess presently, may also change. It is important that you pay attention to

potential changes. Awareness, or lack of awareness, may be the difference in the success or failure of a relationship.

"No, I don't want a person exactly like me. I don't necessarily believe opposites attract either. However, I would like a person that complements me, like puzzle pieces. They are not identical, yet they fit together perfectly."
- Zipporah

Some people believe they can get involved with someone and possibly change them later. Women in particular believe that mind-blowing fellatio and sex will cause a man to change. Attempting to change or train a person to fit your qualifications is futile if they refuse to change. Even if their behavior happens to change, their character, or the core of who they are, may remain constant. However, you can train the relationship and communicate how you want to be treated. But beware, the entire process will be a challenge.

Ultimately, change is inevitable if you plan to coexist in a successful relationship with someone of the opposite sex. If you don't understand this dynamic, you may want to reevaluate if you really want to be in a relationship. However, if you choose wisely, hopefully the sacrifice of change will be worth it. Just remember that men and women view life through varied lenses. Nevertheless, to cultivate prosperous relationships, they must continuously learn how to find a happy medium.

COTTON CANDY

FAIRYTALE

During their adolescent years, psychologically and socially, women are programmed to come of age, get married, and start a family. This concept is reinforced through family, media, religion, and everyday life in general. At a very young age, females are exposed to a *Fairytale* world that usually consists of damsels in distress and heroes with romantic story lines. They often always have a happy ending with the princess and her prince charming riding off into the sunset on a white horse. Guess what? It's a reason these types of stories are characterized as *Fairytales* - they are simply not realistic. These whimsical ideas, rooted in emotion, are quite attractive to many women. Thus, there is an urgency for the *Fairytale* to materialize at a young age.

"Women are in love with the idea of being in love."
- Miguel

We all know there are biological differences between the sexes. Obviously, genitalia and hormones are a major difference. But more importantly, a distinct difference is the mode of reproduction. Biologically, women are born with all the eggs they will ever have. As women age, their eggs also age. Procreation is possible as long as she continues her menstrual cycle. However, the possibility of complications with procreation increases as her eggs get older. The overall health of the woman is also a factor. Thus, *Marriage*, having a baby, and starting a family early rather than later in life are part of her overall goals. Ultimately, the psychology and biology of a woman contributes to the *Fairytale* mindset.

> *"I never adopted the Fairytale mindset. The fact that I never had children didn't bother me as I was the oldest of 7 children. Since my mother was a single parent, I fulfilled the role of child and parent to my 6 siblings. I had to cook, clean, wash clothes, and braid hair. When I became an adult, I decided not to have children, because I had already raised my 6 younger siblings."*
> *- Mildred*

It's debatable whether or not women that achieve their goals of spouse, children, and family have actually fulfilled their vision of success. Regardless, many females believe that the coveted *Fairytale* can come true for them and as a result

they start planning their life accordingly. In general, their plan consists of graduating from college, securing a good job, buying a nice car, being married, and having children by a certain age. Some young ladies even plan their weddings during their adolescent years. They choose the dress, wedding colors, the number of bridesmaids and groomsmen, the cake, the venue, and the honeymoon destination. Of course, the presentation of the wedding *Ring* is at the heart of this entire process.

> *"If people put more emphasis on the Marriage versus the wedding, then maybe people would have more successful Marriages."*
> *- Moe*

The desire for the *Fairytale* is the result of socialization and psychological manipulation. Are you okay with the fact that you are being mentally molested? Dare to be different. Finding true love is possible, just not through a *Fairytale* lens. It's apparent that the traditional way of getting married is not the blueprint for a successful *Marriage*. Understand, a goal for *Marriage* without a plan is essentially a *Fairytale*. There is nothing wrong with believing in a *Fairytale* per se, but allow your *Fairytale* to evolve into a solid plan for success.

"Every Fairytale story ends with a kiss, the couple riding off into the sunset, or Marriage. What I would like to know is, What happens the next day, week, month, year...? Did they stay together? and What does 'happily ever after' really mean?"

- Nzinga

Remember the 7 P's for success, *Prior Proper Planning Prevents Piss Poor Performance*. This mantra for success can be used as a guide in relationships and in life overall. So yes, finding true love and having a family is possible if you plan for it. However, you must also consider a very important variable that is essential to the plan - the Man. Additionally, be aware that the male *Species* views the pursuit or idea of *Marriage* and family somewhat differently than the female. He is not bred in the same way.

"Women create their own realities in relationships."

- Andre

WATERMELON

DOGGY STYLE

Unfortunately for women, most men are not wired with the *Fairytale* concept. They don't necessarily look at *Marriage* as a goal. It's more like if it happens, it happens. It doesn't mean that men don't desire *Marriage*; the male mind just operates a little different than the female mind. Just like women, men are socialized through similar mediums, just in a different way. For instance, the excitement and euphoria that the friends of the bride display are not the same reaction that men generally exemplify for the groom when presented with the same announcement. The narrative usually goes as follows:

The groom is hanging out with his friends after asking his longtime girlfriend to marry him and he says, "Man, she got me. I'm getting married."

Single friend 1 says, "For real?"

Single friend 2 asks, "How does it feel?"

Married friend says, "Don't do it!"

Groom says, "But you're married."

Married friend explains, "That's why I'm telling you not to do it. Enjoy your freedom. They change after you get married. No more head, no more pretty panties..."

> *"Juicy J: Man, don't do it. Don't do it.*
> *Andre 3000: When a man is ready, he's ready. When yawl get 80, 70, 60, 55 years old, you gone be sitting in a rocking chair by yourself. Yawl gone be the only old brothers in the club.*
> *Bun B: All playing aside man, why get married pimping, why?"*
> *- UGK/Outkast, Playa's Anthem*

After the friends finish hazing the newly engaged man, they suggest treating him to a night of strip clubs and spirits to bring him comfort in light of his newly found station in life. Again, it's not that men are insensitive or lack the capacity to show compassion for the opposite sex, they're just built different - biologically and psychologically.

> *"Women may fake orgasms for relationships, but men fake relationships for orgasms."*
> *- Marcus*

The social and biological differences between men and women directly impact how they view *Marriage* and relationships overall. Unlike women, men are not worried about their biological clock because men constantly produce sperm and have the ability to procreate almost indefinitely. A man's biological clock is more mental and spiritual versus biological. Their urgency to procreate may be contingent on their friends having kids or realizing they want to leave a lasting legacy. Ultimately, men are not in a rush to get married, nor are they pressured. If a man is up in age whenever he decides to settle down and have children, he can simply choose a younger woman. For example, some older men that had children with younger women were Ron Isley at 66, Larry King at 66, Jeff Goldblum at 62, and Steve Martin at 67. As men age, their dating pool seems to expand, up or down.

"When a guy calls you hot, he's looking at your body. When a guy calls you pretty, he's looking at your face. When a guy calls you beautiful, he's looking at your heart. All three guys still want to fuck you, though."
- Hector

Psychologically, men could really care less about the *Fairytale*. The ugly truth is that women are viewed more as individual conquests until a man runs across that one woman they can't see themselves without. Ladies don't be fooled, when you meet a man age 8 or 88, I don't care how nice he is, how much of a gentleman he is, and no matter what façade he

presents, trust me when I say, he only has one thing on his mind. He is trying to figure out how many dinners, movies, concerts, and/or conversations it's going to take to get your G-string to hit the floor, get your ankles to touch your ears, beat your back out, knock you off, get dem draws, invade your vaginal walls, get the booty, or whatever colloquial phrase or word used to denote sex. Men are physical creatures and hunters by nature, and initially that's the only thing on their mind. Also, when it comes to sex, in many cases men have zero expectations, whereas women do, especially if the sex is exceptional.

"Yeah, all my bitches love me, and I love all my bitches, but it's like soon as I cum, I come to my senses."
- Lil' Wayne, Love Me

Remember, men put women into two main categories: recreation and *Marriage* material. Don't get discouraged if you've just realized you've been someone's cuddy (recreation). Everybody has been someone's cuddy at least once or twice. The goal is to not be the cuddy for everybody. Now don't get me wrong, a man's initial plan of attack can change contingent on a few variables. It depends on how the woman presents herself, timing, and the number of women in the man's rotation at the time, just to name a few. But more importantly, how she presents herself is key. Unfortunately, sometimes perception is reality.

"*You are out in the bar with your buddies and you see a woman. She looks good, not in that classical way. She's got half her ass hanging out her skirt, titties all mashed together, popping out the top of her turtleneck and shit. You're with your buddies, you've got a couple drinks in you, and it doesn't come out right. 'DAMN, look at them titties!'*

The girl says, 'Wait a minute! Just because I'm dressed this way does not make me a whore!' Which is true. Gentlemen, that is true. Just because they dress a certain way doesn't mean they are a certain way. Don't ever forget it.

But ladies, you must understand that is fucking confusing! It just is. Now that would be like me, Dave Chappelle the comedian, walking down the street in a cop uniform. Somebody might run up on me, saying 'Oh, thank God. Officer, help us! Come on. They're over here. Help us!'

'OHH!! Just because I'm dressed this way does not make me a police officer!'

All right, ladies, fine. You are not a whore. But you are wearing a whore's uniform, I'll tell you that."

- Dave Chappelle Interview

As far as timing, if men are not where they want to be in life, they tend not to desire *Marriage* until they have themselves situated or have satisfied certain goals. It may be a certain level of education, financial stability, or even "sowing their wild

oats." If they have not reached that goal or station, they won't be ready to receive anyone seriously.

"I'm not afraid of commitment, I just don't want to commit to you."
- Fernando

Last, the concept of rotations does not necessarily apply to all men. Before we continue, let me qualify the term "rotation." A rotation is when a man or woman entertains, shares time and space, and or converses with multiple individuals. Being in a rotation does not necessarily denote a sexual relationship. However, with men it usually does. For women, not necessarily the case. A woman's rotation may consist of men that can assist her with varied tasks that may arise. For example, she may have a guy that is a really good mechanic for when she has car trouble, a landscaper to maintain her yard, and a handyman to fix things around her house. Some women even have "sponsors" that are willing to pay a bill or two, take her out to eat, and/or finance an occasional all-inclusive vacation. In most cases, she is only sleeping with one person in her rotation, if that.

"If I could combine everyone in my rotation, I would have the perfect woman."
- Malcolm

Now, when you first meet a guy and it appears that several women are checking for him, if he's very intelligent, charismatic, and charming, and if he has a natural presence, he probably has a rotation. These types of men tend be politicians, pastors, principals, professors, entrepreneurs, professional athletes, entertainers, and other professions where men have a commanding presence. Most women love powerful men. However, women, if you are not prepared to compete, WALK AWAY. These types of men usually do not want to settle down, they're having too much fun. You're probably saying, "Just because he encompasses all or some of the aforementioned qualities, it doesn't necessarily mean he has a rotation." You're absolutely correct. Yet, it is highly probable. Now, you're probably wondering how to determine if you are in a rotation. Here are some indications that you may be in a rotation:

"I didn't mine being in his rotation, because he was in my rotation too."
~Kim

- If there is a pattern of him getting off the phone with you to talk to everyone else that calls.
- If you never meet any of his friends or family.
- If you only see him on certain days.

- If you never see him while you're on your menstrual cycle, but you see him right before or right after your menstrual cycle.
- If he never spends extended periods of time with you.
- When he celebrates holidays, you only see him before or after the holiday.

"You can't give everyone in your rotation the same treatment. Everyone can't believe they are the main person. For example, if a person participates in various holidays, they are not going to want to spend time together the day before or the day after, or a breakfast or lunch date the day of. They are going to want the primetime spot, dinner."
- Donald

If you have experienced any or all of these situations, you might be in a rotation, and yes, some indicators are identical to signs of being "recreation." However, if you have not experienced any or all of these situations, it does not necessarily mean you are not in a rotation. Yes, you could be *Marriage* material, but simultaneously be in a rotation. The reason you may not realize you are in a rotation is because you may be at the top of the rotation and the rest of the pack are recreation, which makes them expendable.

"I love you girl. You got my son and you'll probably be my wife. You want me to be honest? You're my woman. Them

other hoes is tricks. I make love to you, I want to be with you, but I fuck other females from time to time. I don't know why, I just do. That's the situation. You feel better now? That's some honesty for your ass. Deal with it. I love you enough to be honest. I lie 'cause I do love you. Being honest would mean I don't give a fuck. Out on the street, I tell these hoes the truth. I lie to you because I care. It's obvious you can't handle the truth."

- Jodi, Baby Boy

You're probably saying to yourself, "If a man finds a woman that is *Marriage* material, why would he lie, cheat, and subject her to being in a rotation with other women that are only there for recreational purposes, but leave her if she displayed similar behavior?" The short answer is, "Men are full of crap." Not necessarily for wanting to be with multiple women, but more so for the lying and deception. If you feel this behavior is unfair and hypocritical, you're right, it is.

In general, a man may treat various women in his life entirely different. For example, his wife or girlfriend can have the world. She is his queen. The young lady in his life that is recreation and/or in his rotation, never or very rarely gets a movie or dinner, just penis. He doesn't deem her worthy of having anything more. However, this same man will tell his homegirl, daughter, or sister to steer away from situations and

men like him that would possibly treat her in an identical fashion. Crazy, right!?!

"The only thing I have for these hoes is a pack of gum and hard dick and I'm fresh outta of gum."
- Rollo

With all that being said, don't fret, it's not a hopeless situation. You just have to find the right person and situation for you, at the opportune time. But be careful not to marry a man before he's ready. For example, would you prefer to marry an older mature man that has a philandering past and has evolved to the point where he is ready to settle down and be monogamous? Or would you like to marry a younger, seemingly sheltered man that has very little experience in life and with women, yet may have the potential to display a womanizing nature 10 years into the *Marriage* because of curiosity?

"Before I marry a man, I want him to fulfill his every erotic desire. That includes threesomes, orgies, and whatever else he thinks he needs to get out of his system."
- Nikki

The most notorious male whores can fall in love and settle down with a quality woman. The woman he deems as "The One" can penetrate all barriers, but it has to happen organically. He will do whatever it takes to keep this woman, even if it takes going through "hell and high water." However, the relationship cannot be forced and most importantly, do not give him an ultimatum. Allow him to choose you. Don't be overzealous and attempt to put a man in a position of commitment before he is ready. It will not work. If he is not ready, he will either cut his losses and walk away or stay and possible resentment may emerge, which may lead to infidelity. Ultimately, men want to settle down and have a family as well, they may just have a different timetable.

> *"Don't marry a man in his 20s. He is not ready. All men need to get a certain level of 'hoe-ness' out of their system before they get married."*
> *- Omawale*

Once you get past the hard, apprehensive, non-committal exterior of a WORTHY man, he can be the King you always dreamed of. He can be your best friend, lover, father of your children, and provider. Understand, the aforementioned description of how a man thinks and functions is a general overall depiction. All men are not monolithic in their thinking and how they function. When you meet a man, you must assess who and what he is, simultaneously understanding who and what you are. At the center of understanding who and what individuals are as men and women, are historical and present-day gender roles. Whether you agree or not, gender roles

directly affect men and women individually and in relationships.

"I'm a movement by myself. But I'm a force when we're together. Mami I'm good all by myself. But baby you, you make me better...."

- Ne-Yo, Make Me Better

ICE CREAM

ROLE CALL

How are men and women supposed to operate in a relationship? What does it mean to be a gentleman or a lady? Is chivalry an outdated concept? Do women still cook? Why does each gender have to fulfill certain aspects of a relationship as it relates to their anatomy? Why are there such stark differences in people's thinking and functionality as it relates to various areas of male/female interaction? For example, have you ever thought about why men are expected to open doors and pull out chairs for women? Have you wondered why women are supposed to fix a man's plate and iron his clothes? Don't these individuals have the ability to complete these tasks independently? These and similar questions may be answered by looking at the socialization process of gender roles.

Now, ask yourself, do you think gender roles are biological or do you feel men and women have been conditioned to fulfill a particular role? Furthermore, is there a combination of both natural instinct and socialization? Along with knowing what type of person you are and what type of person you are compatible with, you must also understand gender roles, and if and how these roles will be delineated in your personal relationships.

> *"We teach girls to shrink themselves, to make themselves smaller. We say to girls, 'You can have ambition, but not too much. You should aim to be successful, but not too successful. Otherwise you will threaten the man.' Because I am female, I am expected to aspire to Marriage. I am expected to make my life choices always keeping in mind that Marriage is the most important. Now Marriage can be a source of joy and love and mutual support. But why do we teach girls to aspire to Marriage, and we don't teach boys the same? We raise girls to see each other as competitors – not for jobs or for accomplishments, which I think can be a good thing, but for the attention of men. We teach girls that they cannot be sexual beings in the way that boys are."*
> *- Chimamanda Ngozi Adichie*

When you are gazing at newborns in the maternity ward at the hospital, how can you identify the gender? Exactly, the

boys are wrapped in blue blankets and the girls are wrapped in pink blankets. Yes, the anatomy you were born with determined the blanket that encapsulated you at birth. Thus, the socialization of gender roles has begun. At the same time, the baby is usually assigned a gender appropriate name or a unisex name.

Gender Role Origins

From day one, when children are born they are assigned a gender, boy or girl, and are socialized to conform to varied roles solely based on their biological sex. Gender roles are based on standards or societal norms created by society. In many cultures, feminine roles are usually associated with subservience, nurturing, and passivity. Masculinity is associated with aggression, strength, and dominance. As stated earlier, overall socialization starts at birth. Gender socialization also starts at birth, and is influenced by the five major agents of socialization: Family, Education, Community, Peer Groups, and Mass Media.

During those early years, parents provide female children with dress up paraphernalia and toy dolls that cultivate role play, social proximity, and nurturing. Male children receive toy guns, superhero action figures, and trucks which stimulate aggression, solitary play, and motor skills. The effects of early gender role socialization remain very prevalent later in life. In

the professional world, women tend to move toward careers such as healthcare, education, social work, and childcare. Males tend to be more dominant in areas of law enforcement, politics, construction, and the military. These gender roles also carry over into relationships and *Marriage*.

Historical Gender Roles

Generally speaking, in various cultures across the world, men were the warriors and hunters, and women were the gatherers who took care of the home and children. Over time that narrative has evolved somewhat. There is a general consensus in American history that the feminist movement and the current trend of female gender roles evolved during World War II. As a result of many men leaving for the war, there was a shortage of workers to work in various fields. Factories in particular experienced significant shortages. Most factories provided the American military the artillery needed to protect the countries' interests worldwide. As a result, women that were once stay-at-home moms were thrust into the industrial workforce. Some women were eager to work and wanted to do their part to defend their country, while others were not as willing to go work in the factories. This era was represented by an iconic female character known as *Rosie the Riveter*, a White woman wearing a bandana, sleeves rolled up, and muscles flexed.

"Feminist: the person who believes in the social, political, and economic equality of the sexes."
- Chimamanda Ngozi Adichie

However, the aforementioned assertion is actually somewhat of a misnomer. There were certain women that always worked and/or had a presence in the American workforce. Most of these women were in the societal lower class, and many were women of color. For example, during the inception of the United States and prior, the enslavement of Africans was accepted and legal. Therefore, African women were working side-by-side with African men for centuries. After slavery was abolished, there was sharecropping. This trend of women working continued throughout the 19th and 20th centuries with women of color and women from the lower classes serving as nannies and maids.

"Black women struggle to identify with traditional feminism because they do not identify with the issues that feminism typically advocates."
- Clenora Hudson-Weems & Alicia Boisnier

Unlike their White middle and upper-class female peers, African women did not have the "luxury" of staying at home to "take care of their children and be housewives." Ironically, the women that were the so-called housewives; who were supposed to be raising their own children and fulfilling their motherly and

wifely duties of cooking and cleaning; hired Black women to do those jobs. This practice was depicted in movies such as *The Help,* starring Viola Davis and *The Long Walk Home*, starring Whoopi Goldberg. Both movies showed how Black women spent their lives as nannies and maids, taking care of prominent White families. These working women were not treated with dignity or respect and therefore they were not glorified or recognized as working women.

Therefore, when you hear or read about feminism in the context of the role of women in the family structure (which was primarily to take care of the home, children, and various domestic tasks) and the man's role of earning an income outside of the home (to take care of all the family expenses), understand that this did not apply to everyone. It only applied to individuals that were considered to be the true citizens of America, the White population.

In response to a feminist movement that was mainly led by middle-class heterosexual White women, who were advocating for social change related to gender-based oppression while ignoring race and class-based oppression, arose womanism. Poet and author Alice Walker is credited with coining the term "womanist." Womanism is a social theory deeply rooted in the gender-based and racial oppression of Black women.

At the core of womanism is a social change perspective based on the daily trials and tribulations of Black women and other women of color. Additionally, the womanist movement seeks techniques to not just eradicate inequalities of Black women, but for all individuals, regardless of color. They also desire a society where men and women can coexist, while maintaining their cultural identity. With the inclusion of men as a component of womanism, womanists have the opportunity to address gender oppression without seemingly attacking males.

> *"The womanish girl exhibits willful, courageous, and outrageous behavior that is considered to be beyond the scope of societal norms. Additionally, a womanist is a woman who loves another woman, sexually and/or non-sexually. She appreciates and prefers women's culture, women's emotional flexibility...[she] is committed to the survival and wholeness of an entire people, male and female. Not a separatist, except periodically for health...loves the spirit....loves struggle. Loves herself. Regardless."*
> *- Alice Walker*

While some argued that the social structure of historical gender roles was sexist, others explained that the system exemplified a division of labor where different segments of

society simply performed varied types of labor. With various entities deeming these practices unfair and oppressive, the tide started to change with the first of four waves of feminism.

The first wave of feminism appeared in the late 19th and early 20th century, and was inspired by global politics and industrialization. The main focus of the movement at that time was to create opportunities for women with a focus on suffrage. Ultimately, women gained the right to vote in 1920 with the passing of the 19th amendment. Not only were women fighting for the right to vote, other rights encompassed the right not to lose their children in marital conflicts, the right to an education, the right not to be property of their husbands or fathers, the right to a divorce, the right to the money they earned when they worked, and the overall right to work and to work in a safe environment.

In its infant stages, feminism was intertwined with abolitionist and temperance movements, which gave a voice to women such as Susan B. Anthony and Sojourner Truth, the latter who famously demanded, "Ain't I a woman?" In conjunction with the feminist movement, the anti-racism movement was simultaneously gaining traction. Both movements supported each other in protest against the White male dominant system of misogyny and racism.

ROLE CALL

The second wave of feminism appeared in the 1960s amidst the civil rights and anti-war (Vietnam War) movements, and the growing self-consciousness of various interest groups worldwide. The movement of the second wave was increasingly radical and the dominant issues represented in this phase comprised of reproductive rights and sexuality. The majority of the movement's energy was geared toward passing the Equal Rights Amendment to the constitution, which guaranteed equal rights, no matter the sex. In addition, the second wave also focused on the woman's role as mother and wife, capitalism, patriarchy, and normative heterosexuality.

"Feminism is not just about women; it's about letting all people lead fuller lives."
- Jane Fonda

Being that the second wave was among many other anti-establishment movements, it was easily dismissed by some as less important than the efforts to stop the Vietnam War and the Black Power Movement. In contrast to the first wave; which in general was propelled by Western middle class White women; the second wave attracted new blood in the form of women of color and women from developing countries pursuing solidarity and sisterhood. Additionally, women of the second wave professed that women's struggle for equal rights was not only a gender struggle, but a class struggle. Ultimately, this

wave of feminism attempted to rid society of sexism in its entirety.

"I think women are foolish to pretend they are equal to men. They are far superior and always have been. Whatever you give a woman, she will make greater. If you give her sperm, she will give you a baby. If you give her a house, she will give you a home. If you give her groceries, she will give you a meal. If you give her a smile, she will give you her heart. She multiplies and enlarges what is given to her. So, if you give her any crap, be ready to receive a ton of shit!"
- William Golding, British Novelist, Playwright & Poet

The third wave of feminism materialized in the early 1990s and was stimulated by post-modern and post-colonial logic. The focus of this wave was female sexual freedom. These freedoms included, but were not limited to being able to not only identify sexual desires, but to also freely express those desires without judgment. An interesting aspect of this phase was the pushback to the first and second wave. Women of the previous two waves were perplexed by the young feminist's readopting of symbols they believed to be connected with male oppression, such as showing cleavage, high heels, and lip stick. Ironically, many third wave feminists refuse to identify with the term "feminist," because they feel it's limited in scope.

"They call us sluts and whores all the time, so we just embrace it. I have slut written across my vagina."
- Amber Rose

The most current development in the feminist movement is the fourth wave of feminism. The definition and overall framework of the term is somewhat ambiguous. There are minority advocates that campaign for incorporating a combination of justice with religious spirituality. Most feminists of the fourth wave tend to focus on the technological components of the movement. Fourth wave feminism is often associated with online feminism, leveraging Twitter, Facebook, YouTube, and other forms of social media which support, communicate, and activate social justice and gender equality.

The fourth wave is symbolic of the continuing influence of the third wave, with its focus on the politics of challenging the presence of sexism and misogyny in the daily rhetoric of television and literature, advertising, media, and film. This aspect of online feminism has influenced companies to closely monitor their marketing campaigns so that they are not targeted for sexism in their advertisements. In addition to online feminism, the fourth wave has been associated with more focus on intersectionality, including unity with other social justice movements and the rejection of trans-exclusionary radical

feminism. Fourth-wave feminism stands on the shoulders of the first three waves. What sets this wave apart from the others are broader ideas of equal rights and the addition of more advanced technology.

It's debatable whether or not a woman can have a successful career and a successful *Marriage* and family. There are certain segments of society that feel that women's liberation and the rise of the feminist movement has negatively impacted *Marriages* in society. Others feel that the feminist movement was not for all women, at least not early on, as it relates to race and social class. The aforementioned statements may be contentious; however, the one fact that cannot be denied is that the feminist movement has caused a seismic shift in the dynamics of relationships and *Marriages* as it relates to gender roles.

"Feminism killed chivalry."
- Manny

As gender roles evolved, *Marriages* experienced differences from how roles were historically fulfilled. Before gender roles started to evolve, the roles of men and women were clearly delineated. Men went to work, made all the money, satisfied outside chores, and paid all the bills, generally speaking. Women were responsible for cooking, cleaning, laundry, taking care of all the children's needs, and still had to

have enough energy to take care of their husband's sexual needs after he came home from work.

In the 21ˢᵗ century, gender roles for many *Marriages* look a little different than what once was. Presently, there are more women in American society that are career oriented and generating their own income, making more than their husbands in some cases. Thus, instead of having a one income household, the household has two incomes to support the family. Sounds good, right? It all depends on your perspective. Think about it for a minute. If both parents are working all day, who's supervising the children? Whose teaching them? Who's influencing them the most? Some would say, "That's the function of nurseries and nannies." Once the role of the female, now becomes the responsibility of a non-familial person.

The question is not whether gender roles are right or wrong, the question is, are gender roles right or wrong for you and your situation? Whether you agree or not, even though many women are pursuing careers, if they have a family, more times than not, they are still expected to fulfill their traditional motherly and wifely duties once they get home. Some have identified these duties as the second shift. Is that fair? Let's look at some possible pros and cons of traditional versus non-traditional gender roles in a *Marriage*.

Traditional Roles

Pros

The roles are definitive and there is rarely ever a question of who is responsible for various aspects of the relationship and family.

The kids will be raised and mostly influenced by a biological parent versus a caretaker.

The family can possibly have daily home cooked meals for breakfast, lunch, and dinner versus eating out.

The household would/should be clean daily, because the woman is home all day.

The woman has an abundance of time to nurture her children and husband.

The woman doesn't have to worry about financial security. Her security is provided by her husband.

Cons

The man generates the only income and the woman relies on him financially.

The man may feel that since he generates the income, he has no other responsibilities as it relates to the household or children.

The woman may grow tired of being at home and just having conversations with children.

The woman may feel she is treated unfairly by her counterpart, because the man seems to possess the most power.

The woman doesn't have an identity. She is simply the wife of…or the mother of…, thus the woman may eventually want more.

"Well, I'm old fashioned and I want a man like my grandfather that's going to take care of me."
- Carol

Non-Traditional Roles

Pros

The household has two incomes versus one income.
With additional income and resources, parents are able to do more for their children, monetarily speaking.
The woman is not entirely relying on her husband for financial support because she has her own career and generates her own income.

Cons

With two parents working all day, the children are being supervised by someone else.
When the *Marriage* is presented with various problems that may lead to the demise of the relationship and family, the woman may elect to leave the *Marriage* immediately, since she may generate the same or more income than her husband, versus no income in the past.
A career woman, in many cases, still must fulfill her "motherly role," whereas a man's role is unchanged for the most part. The woman may become burned out.

Old Fashioned

The pros and cons of traditional versus non-traditional roles may vary with each person and each relationship. What is your preference? Even though it's the 21st century and women have more options than they had in the past, you may still want to fulfill the traditional roles of a woman. Additionally, you

51

may want to be careful in seeking men that you think are like your grandfather, because you don't necessarily know the whole story about your grandfather and your grandparents as a whole. You only know the story you were given.

> *"I'm old fashioned, I never pay for dates. If you want this pussy, you have to spend some money. There's no romance without finance."*
> *- Charlotte*

When they were dating, you were told your grandfather courted your grandmother and treated her like a queen. She never paid for one date. You know the part about your grandmother never having to work, your grandfather paying all the bills, and your grandmother devoting all her time to raising her children properly and having the option to work a part-time job at her leisure. However, the part of the story you weren't privy to is the one about him having another family across town, which no one knew about until he died. You were devastated to see these adult children at the funeral that resembled your father and his siblings. He was a great provider, but he also felt that he "paid the cost to be the boss" and he could do whatever he wanted to do as long as his family was taken care of.

> *"I'll be back. Don't wait up."*
> *- Papa Wyatt*

New Millennium Woman

Let's say you see yourself as a "new millennium woman" that's head strong and independent, and feel entirely equal to your male counterpart. Are you sure you want to be treated and viewed as an equal? Let's see how that may play out. As far as dating, you would pay for dinners, movies, trips, and other activities equally. In a *Marriage*, all bills would be paid equally by both parties. As far as opening doors and pulling out chairs, the female and male would show acts of chivalry to each other equally.

"Women want to be independent and equal until the waiter brings the check to the table."
-Angela

Maybe you want a bit of both worlds. You want the provider and the security. At the same time, you want the freedom to do what you want to do when you want to do it. Your preference is that the man pays all the bills and sponsors all activities and outings, with the option of spending your own money on yourself. In addition, you expect your man to be chivalrous. You want all the benefits of traditional and non-traditional gender roles, but none of the drawbacks. Is this fair? How is the man benefiting from this relationship? How long will this type of relationship last? Will there be resentment as a

result of this type of arrangement? Maybe a balance of power would be beneficial for both parties to foster a healthier union.

> *"A variation of gender roles would probably work better for me. For example, if I arrived home from work before my wife, I wouldn't wait for her to get home for my family and I to eat. That's not fair or logical. I would cook, make sure the kids complete their homework, eat dinner, and take their baths. Once my wife gets home, she will discover that the house is clean, the kids are asleep, her dinner is in the microwave, and tomorrow's lunch is in the refrigerator. She only has to do one thing - take off her panties and assume the position."*
> *- T'Challa*

Situations and scenarios will certainly play out differently for various individuals and situations. It's contingent on how a person was raised, one's level of education, life exposure, and what lens in which they view relationships. One version may work in a certain situation with a particular person, but is altogether different under other circumstances with someone else. Additionally, a relationship may adopt and practice a version of gender roles initially and change over a period of time depending on the circumstances of the relationship. The bottom line is that you must figure out what version of gender roles are most optimal for your situation and station in life, and what will benefit your quality of life the best.

"His money is our money and my money is my money."
- Ivanka

Moreover, both men and women must understand the polar differences between each other, and the universal *Double Standards* adopted by society as social norms. These *Double Standards* may not be as flexible as gender roles. Unfortunately, even though men and women are striving to work together in successful relationships, the rules may vary on occasion.

PLAYING FOR THE RING

CANDY APPLE

DOUBLE STANDARDS

We have identified distinct differences between men and women and how they view relationships per gender roles. Unfortunately, sometimes these differences cause division versus unification amongst the sexes, because in too many cases, males and females choose to give opposition more consideration than the commonalities they share. Another point of contention between the sexes is societal *Double Standards*.

Double Standards are principles or a code of morals adopted by society that apply differently and usually more rigorously to one group of people or circumstances than to another, in an unfair fashion. *Double Standards* related to gender are established at a very early age, starting with how males and females are raised. Boys seemingly get more freedom than girls during their adolescent years. A male's independence is encouraged. They have later curfews and

parents generally don't have a problem with them dating at an early age. In many cases males are encouraged to interact with girls, because "quiet as it's kept," most parents want to confirm that their sons are heterosexual. On the other hand, parents tend to want to shelter their daughters. They tell them to keep their legs closed and abstain from having sex until they get married. Is that fair? Are *Double Standards* a byproduct of gender roles?

"My mother always expressed that she never wanted girls because girls would want to wear her jewelry, make-up, and clothes. She also said that girls get pregnant. Whenever people would say, 'well, boys get girls pregnant,' her reply was, 'that's fine but the baby won't be in my house.'"
~ Julia

People from some schools of thought feel that some *Double Standards* are not just unfair, but sexist. While I agree that *Double Standards* on the surface are unfair, they seem to balance each other out. Balance in the sense that sometimes *Double Standards* benefit the male and sometimes they benefit the female. Let's examine various areas of life where *Double Standards* may be quarrelsome as it relates to male/female interaction. We will examine *Double Standards* that generally benefit men first.

DOUBLE STANDARDS

Promiscuity

One of the most common and popular grudges I hear from women relates to the promiscuous activities of men and how the perception of men and women differ even though their actions are identical. This is very true. Men can have sex with a multitude of women without acquiring a negative stigma and in many cases this behavior is considered to be manly. Women, on the other hand, who display identical promiscuous behavior are labeled whores, cuddy, hookers, and street booty.

> *"A key that opens many locks is called a master key. A lock that is opened by many keys is a shitty lock."*
> *- Donnie*

Even though it's unfair, this behavior is accepted by men and women. Ultimately, this womanizer can still marry a quality woman one day. Oddly, in some situations, a man having the reputation as a "ladies man" is attractive to certain females. A woman conversely, who has a questionable history of sleeping with a variety of men has a more challenging task of marrying a quality suitor. It's possible, but challenging, especially if the man knows about her sordid past. This man can get married and still maintain his philandering lifestyle. What makes you think he was going to change? Typically, women are not able to get away with the same routine. "Why," you ask? Women tend to be a lot more forgiving, while men on the other

hand, are not. Additionally, a man cannot conceive the idea of their woman and another man doing anything sexual. If she cheats, it's over.

"Young hoes grow up to be old hoes."
- Jerome

Alphas

Alphas have Type A personalities, are very assertive, and direct. When men have a Type A personality, they are admired and celebrated. They are considered born leaders. Women that display similar characteristics are unfairly characterized as a bitch. Traditionally, being assertive and headstrong is a masculine trait and women displaying those traits are not always perceived in a positive light.

Marriage

As it relates to *Marriage*, men may choose to marry at any time, young or old without any pressure from society, family, or friends. Women unfortunately are not afforded the same luxury. This phenomenon is impacted by a woman's biological clock and societal pressures for women to marry at an early age. Also, men seem to be able to marry or date women that are significantly younger, whereas women seem to experience more scrutiny. Now, let's examine *Double Standards* that benefit women.

DOUBLE STANDARDS ☾

"A man can get married anytime he chooses. A woman has to wait until she is asked."
- Carolyn W. Rosemond

Dating

The benefits yielded from *Double Standards* differ for women. On a very superficial level, females receive free drinks, meals, shows, trips, money, and extravagant gifts from men that are in pursuit of their company, more specifically sex. In general, the woman is the prize and holds all the power, so it may seem. Many women not only seem to accept this *Double Standard*, they encourage it. Some people may even perceive this behavior as a woman monetizing her vagina, figuratively and literally speaking.

"I don't pay for dates. Especially not the first date. If a man can't take me out and pay for a meal and then expect to get some pussy, he is not the man for me."
- Goldie

Domestic Violence

Whenever there is a verbal or physical confrontation between the sexes and the authorities are involved, in most cases the man is penalized because men are characterized as the stronger of two sexes, physically. Thus, men are expected to deescalate confrontations with women, not retaliate. From a very young age, males are taught not to hit females, under any

circumstances. If a man elects to engage into a physical altercation with a woman, he is in a no win situation, regardless of who is at fault. Even seeking help for domestic violence is biased. Women generally have a multitude of resources to access if they experience domestic violence. On the contrary, if a man experiences domestic violence from a girlfriend or wife, he's not taken seriously. It's not common, but it happens.

Procreation

When it comes to procreation outside of *Marriage*, the woman holds all the power. Whether the man wants the child or not, it's the woman's ultimate decision to get an abortion or not. Even if a man feels he should have some input on this life changing decision, many women feel that no one should have any control over their bodies. In some cases, the woman may not even want to give the child the last name of the father because they are not married to him.

> *"I carried this child for 9 months and we are not married. You actually think MY child is going to have your last name?"*
>
> *- Yaya*

Also, as far as procreation is concerned, if a woman has aspirations of going to a sperm bank because she's an *Independent Woman* who wants a baby without *Marriage*, it tends to be accepted. She can anonymously choose her sperm donor and raise her child with no potential interference from the father. Whereas, if a man wants a surrogate mother because *Marriage* is not the route he wants to take, it's somewhat frowned upon. There is also the potential of the surrogate to develop an attachment during the pregnancy, which may be a problem. People tend to feel that a child needs their mother more than their father. This also seems to be the case when it comes to adoption by a single parent.

Sex

If a man wants to have sex with his wife or significant other and she rejects his advances because she is tired, has a headache, or is just simply not in the mood, her actions are deemed acceptable. Not necessarily popular, but acceptable and authorized, because a woman has the right to say no, right? However, when the shoe is on the other foot, the rules are not applied in the same fashion. If the woman wants to have sex and the man rejects her advances, all hell breaks loose. All types of accusations are made. He's either having sex with someone else or he is gay. A man can't possibly not be in the mood for intercourse. All men want to have sex all the time, right?

Sexuality

Sexuality can be a controversial subject overall. For some it's black and white for both sexes. Others see it as a different

set of rules for men versus women. It goes back to those societal norms. Female homosexuality and bisexuality seems more accepted than male homosexuality and bisexuality. Some men even look at woman on woman sex as an arousing thought. Ask a man what his biggest sexual fantasy is and in most cases, it will be to have a threesome (two women, one man). Before you ask, "What about two men and one woman?" Two men and one woman constitutes a "train" (gang bang), not a threesome, because the men do not touch each other. All three parties interacting constitutes a threesome. Women tend to view man on man sex as a repulsive thought and they do not want to see it.

"I thought about how it would be to be with a woman, but I would never go through with it."
- Cheryl

Some women even have the luxury of experimenting with both sexes until they determine what they are more comfortable with, or they just choose to interact with both sexes before deciding to get married. Women can even go to female strip clubs and pay for lap dances without judgment. Men that attempt the same path are not equally accepted. Are you skeptical? Let's look at the following scenarios. Both scenarios are of a couple having a conversation the night before their wedding. They are having a discussion about being transparent and honest about their sexual history before they move forward with this life changing experience. In Scenario A, the woman is confessing. In Scenario B, the male is confessing.

Scenario A

Her: "Hey babe, I have something I want to share with you."

Him: "What's up!?!"

Her: "Before we make this huge decision to be together for the rest of our lives, I need you to know something about my past."

Him: "You weren't born a man, were you? Just playing! Okay, I'm listening. It can't be that bad."

Her: "Wheeew! Okay, here we go. You remember my roommate from college, Felicia?"

Him: "Yeah, the one with the big booty!"

Her: "Yes, her. Well, when we were in undergrad, we went out and got really drunk at this fraternity party."

Him: "What's wrong with that?"

Her: "Wait, I'm not finished."

Him: "Oookay."

Her: "After we got back to our dorm room, we made out and went down on each other. It only happened once and it hasn't happened since."

Him: "That's it!?! What's Felicia's number? (Laughter) I'm just playing, unless…I'm just playing. I can't wait to marry you tomorrow."

Scenario B

Him: "Hey boo, I have something I want to share with you."

Her: "Sure, what's up!?!"

Him: "Before we make this huge decision to be together for the rest of our lives, I need you to know something about my past. It's important that you hear this from me."

Her: "Okay, I'm listening. It can't be that bad. Whatever it is, I will still love you."

Him: "Wheeew! Okay, here we go. You remember my roommate from college, Alonzo?"

Her: "Yeah, the fine one that use to play in the NFL! Man, he had sex with all my sorority sisters!"

Him: "Yes, him. Well, when we were in undergrad, we went out and got really drunk at this homecoming party."

Her: "What's wrong with that?"

Him: "Wait, I'm not finished."

Her: "Oookay."

Him: "After we got back to our apartment, all I remember is passing out on the sofa. The next morning, I woke up nude with semen on my chest and his penis in my mouth."

Her: "What the fuck!?!

Him: "I promise, it only happened once and it hasn't happened since. I don't even remember exactly what happened. I'm pretty sure I didn't enjoy it."

Her: "Are you fucking kidding me? Kill yo'self! You nasty son of a bitch. Why did you wait to tell me this shit the night before our wedding? On top of that, you still hang out with this dude. I knew there was something suspect about him, always getting his eyebrows waxed and shit. Get out of my fucking face. The wedding is off!"

There may be a small percentage of women that will accept a man with a homosexual or bisexual past, but for most women it will create a mental block that will prevent them from cultivating any type of romantic relationship.

"I think some women experiment with other women sexually out of curiosity. I feel that's okay. However, men experimenting with other men sexually is unacceptable. I don't care if they penetrate a man's man-gina (male anus) or if their dookie chute has been penetrated one time, it's absolutely no coming back."
- Charisse

Divorce

In the case of divorce and child custody, many times the woman receives custody of the children, no matter which

parent is the most responsible, which includes financial child support and alimony. Additionally, the man is relegated to only seeing his children every other weekend and holidays. In rare cases where the man receives custody and the woman has a higher salary, if the man requests child support and alimony, he's perceived as a weak man. Is this fair? Absolutely not! Is it reality? Unfortunately, in many situations for the man, it is.

Double Standards are not meant to necessarily be fair. *Double Standards* are dichotomous and hypocritical by nature and are more of a caveat. *Double Standards* are also unwritten agreements accepted by society that you can choose to accept or reject. Now, if you choose not to accept said standards, you must be prepared to face the reality of your decision. Whether you agree or disagree with the *Double Standards* of men and women, being aware of these standards may be beneficial before you decide to enter into any type of romantic relationship, including *Marriage*. In addition to being aware of *Double Standards*, another area of human behavior you may want to investigate before you say, "I Do" is the concept of infidelity and how various individuals may qualify cheating.

PINEAPPLES

SIDE PIECE

Having a *Side Piece* or cheating is a polarizing topic in the relationship world. Some may argue that men having women outside of their union is acceptable and no different than the previously discussed *Double Standards*. I'm sure many women and some men that are reading these words would unequivocally disagree and declare that cheating for both parties is wrong. However, the consensus of some men is that cheating is authorized as long as everyone understands their role, and he takes care of home.

> *"When a man cheats, gets caught, and is forgiven, he thinks he got away with something. He's sadly mistaken. He simply gave his wife a 'free penis card,' which she will gladly play one day, when he least expects it."*
> *- Pimpin Mack*

The question you're probably asking is, "Why do men cheat?" Again, in general, the men that decide to cheat don't necessarily have to have a reason to cheat. Men that decide to cheat step out for various reasons including, but not limited to: boredom, not feeling appreciated, thinking the grass is greener on the other side, or just trying to see if they still got it. In many cases men simply cheat for sport, like playing a game of pool, participating in a pick-up game of basketball, or hunting deer on a full stomach. A man can have the perfect woman at home and still cheat.

> "God
> Come in God
> God come in God
> Damn you're a girl
> Well, I guess the reason why I'm talking to you tonight is
> Cause I've been doing a lot of thinking and
> I consider myself a pretty cool guy
> And I've never cheated on any of my girlfriends
> Well, well except that one little time in Japan but
> That was just some head, and head don't count right?
> Ah, thanks God I knew you'd understand"
> - Andre Benjamin, God (Interlude)

Men tend to have the capability to participate in emotionally detached sex and keep it moving. To quote boxing

terminology, men tend to "stick and move." Additionally, some men don't even deem various types of interactions with other women as cheating. These interactions encompass conversations, in person and on the phone, intimate e-mails, and I know you're not going to believe this, but yes, fellatio. Their rational is, "Well, I didn't have sex with her, so that does not constitute cheating." I know it doesn't make sense to you. You have to speak the language of penis and have a penis to understand.

"I did not have sexual relations with that woman."
- Bill Clinton

So, you're probably saying, "If men are going to cheat or have a *Side Piece*, why get married in the first place?" I agree. That is a very valid question. I've found that the reasons that men marry, even though they know they are going to cheat going into the *Marriage* is multilayered. It may encompass wanting to have children, presenting a certain family façade for appearances because of their career, and/or maybe they procreated with a female acquaintance accidently and they refuse to be a part-time father, so they choose to marry her.

Ironically, in some cases, the *Side Piece's* position is solidified before the wife's position is established. I know, you're probably asking, "Why not just marry the woman that's the *Side Piece*?" Short answer, she is not considered to be

Marriage material. Again, men put women in two categories, recreation and *Marriage* material. You're probably asking, "Don't these women want more?" Maybe, maybe not. Regardless, in most cases men seldom leave their wives and family for the *Side Piece*.

Even if their *Marriage* happens to end in divorce where the man has a *Side Piece*, more times than not, her position will not change. If he chooses to marry again, he will marry someone new. The *Side Piece* will remain the *Side Piece* except in rare cases. Remember, a *Side Piece* is a *Side Piece* is a *Side Piece*. Now, you may ask, "Do all men cheat?" Absolutely not, however, the irony of the monogamous man that does not cheat is that he is the one that experiences a woman cheating on him. Surprise, surprise, women cheat too! The difference is that women just do it better! A whole lot better!

> *"Don't you think for two seconds that if you keep breaking this woman's heart, your sweet, innocent, little, sweet loving, darling woman; she eventually will go out and fuck someone else."*
> - Eddie Murphy, Raw

Some men are under the misconception that having a *Side Piece*, lying, and/or cheating is a lifestyle that is exclusive to men only and is a *Double Standard* that solely benefits the man. A womanizing man is also under the impression that if he takes

care of home, and he is meeting all the sexual needs of his mate, his woman won't dare mimic similar behavior. If a man believes this line of thinking, he's delusional. Not only does she have the proclivity to get her own *Side Piece*, when she decides to pull that trigger, she will be more methodical and calculated about how she cheats versus her male counterpart. Women are craftier and lie better than men. Additionally, women generally have different reasons as to why they step out on their relationship.

> *"Men lie the most. Women tell the biggest lies. Men, we lie all the time. We lie so much it's damn near a language. To call a man out for lying is like playing basketball with a retarded kid and calling him for double-dribble. You gotta let some shit slide. We lie all the time. You know what a man's lie is like? 'I was at Tony's house. I'm at Kenny's house.' That's a man's lie. A women's lie is like, 'It's yo baby.'"*
> *- Chris Rock, Bigger and Blacker*

Cheating or having outside relationships is not a decision that many married women take lightly or even entertain at all. In general, women are very loyal. If a woman has a good man at home, in most cases she will not participate in an extramarital affair. However, there are some women that may cheat for sport, but it's not very common. A female that loves her husband and family, considers her family to be her number one

priority. She does not want to do anything to jeopardize the sanctity of her family unit. However, if chinks in the armor arise from the actions of her mate or simply from growing in totally different directions, the female may have a change in her thinking as it relates to infidelity.

> *"A woman can run farther with her dress up than a man with his pants down."*
> *- Papa Dubb*

The all-encompassing reason a woman may cheat is because she settled and married the wrong person. Specifically, the seven areas or situations that may motivate a woman to entertain the idea of a potential *Side Piece* are infidelity, health issues, negligence, growing apart, pure boredom (mentally, physically, spiritually), wanting variety, or simply not marrying "The One." All the aforementioned areas contribute to various levels of resentment, which may lead to confrontations and infidelity. You're probably saying, "Hey, that would never happen to me. I would just get a divorce before I cheat on my husband. I'm not that type of woman." Let's see how it may play out in these seven areas.

> *"Never say what you will never do."*
> *- Gayle*

Infidelity

You're only going to tolerate nude e-mail pics, 3 A.M. phone calls, motel receipts, late nights with the "homies," and a man not wearing his wedding *Ring* but for so long. You may not leave your man; however, you may possibly seek the attention of an outside admirer to fill the void created by a husband that is redirecting his time and resources toward his *Side Piece* or pieces. You will justify one, two, or three…casual, occasional indiscretions, because compared to his countless affairs, what you do or will do is inconsequential.

"Ladies don't be too upset about your man not wearing his wedding Ring. A man wearing a wedding Ring gets more attention from women than a single man. A married man will go to a bar and converse with a young lady and may even buy her a couple of drinks. Once he is ready to go home, he will pay his tab and attempt be on his way. The young lady he was conversing with, who was hit on by every other guy at the bar is gob smacked by the fact that this man did not try to holla at her. The married man is not pressed. He has booty (his wife) at home. Ultimately, she engages him before he leaves. Her ego would not allow him to get away."
- Latonya

Health Issues

When you initially met each other, you were young, vibrant, and you felt invincible. You ate and drank whatever you wanted without consequence. As you aged, your bodies could not process unhealthy food choices, which led to your husband developing various preventable diseases, specifically high blood pressure. The doctor warned you both in previous years that he was in danger of developing this condition, because not only was it hereditary, he also had very bad eating habits and led an increasingly sedentary lifestyle. As the years went by and habits were unchanged, his condition worsened. Ultimately, what the physician predicted came to fruition. He develops preventable diseases such as high cholesterol, diabetes, and high blood pressure. As a side effect of the diabetes and high blood pressure medication, he experiences erectile dysfunction. Not only can he not perform sexually, he also has no desire to engage in any type of intimacy. His libido is non-existent.

"I haven't had sex in 9 years. My husband has high blood pressure and diabetes. The medication he takes causes him to experience erectile dysfunction. He refuses to change his diet and workout. How long am I supposed to wait to have sex?"
- Latisha

SIDE PIECE

No problem, right? With you being the loyal, committed, and dedicated wife, you are going to do everything in your power to make sure your significant other's health improves. So, you make an executive decision to make sure your family eats better and becomes more active. You rid your home of everything unhealthy and stock it with healthy food choices. This includes fresh fruits and vegetables, fish, and organic chicken. You also procure a family membership at the local fitness center so that your family can get in shape and cultivate a healthier lifestyle together.

Unfortunately, your husband rejects all your efforts. He not only refuses to make healthier choices, he demands that you replace the healthy items with his usual unhealthy choices. He is also adamant about not going to the gym or working out at all. Because of his health issues and the rejection of remedies that could rectify his condition, his erectile dysfunction persists and thus you don't have intercourse or intimacy for the next three years. After three years of no human sexual contact, masturbation and sex toys are not as satisfying anymore. Thus, infidelity is justified and you go out and find a young dude at the local university that runs five miles every day and drinks wheat grass juice. You tried, right?

"Complacency is the enemy of achievement."
- Dennis Kimbro

Negligence

You thought you hit the jackpot when you married the big-time athlete, politician, hustler, pastor, entertainer, military officer, or business man. Life is great, right? You had your *Fairytale* wedding and you have your multiple karat diamond *Ring*. You live in your dream house, you drive your dream car, and you don't want for anything. However, your husband is so successful and in such high demand that he seldom has time to spend at home with his family. He's always away. You spend many of your anniversaries and birthdays alone, and attend various special events without him. Even though you have all the material desires you could imagine, seeing and spending time with your husband is non-existent.

> *"He's rich, he is rich! He's got his own money. And baby when I say he got his own money, I mean the boy has got his own money!"*
> *- Cleo McDowell, Coming to America*

When he finally comes home, he pays you very little attention. He doesn't even notice the little things like you cutting and coloring your hair, wearing a new fragrance, or the fact that you have lost a significant amount of weight after having his second child. But guess who does notice, a past boyfriend that found you on social media, and/or that attractive co-worker that always has nothing but complimentary things to

say to you with each encounter. It was no problem to resist these temptations, until you started feeling like a lonely single mother that was experiencing physical, mental, and spiritual neglect. To fill those voids, you start to justify and entertain those temptations.

"Women tend to find very creative ways to get out of the house. This married woman I used to deal with would tell her husband she was going to the grocery store to get out of the house to come see me. She would come over and get her 15 to 20-minute fix, and then go to the grocery store. She waited to go by the grocery store after she left me, just in case her husband checked the time on the receipt. She made sure to cover all her bases. She was so good, it was scary."
- Todd

Growing Apart

When you married your husband, you thought you were making the most sensible choice. You thought he had everything you were looking for in a man, well at least the most important things you wanted at the time. When you first married each other you had certain needs, wants, and expectations. As you evolved, your needs, wants, and expectations also evolved. Unfortunately, he wasn't paying attention.

 PLAYING FOR THE RING

"What turned me on in my 20s is not the same thing that turns me on in my 30s. I need something more."
- Monica

Boredom

You wanted to travel more, read more books, and try new things sexually. However, your significant other did not change. He is the exact same person he was the day you met him and he refuses to grow on any level. He is a good person who goes to work every day, comes home on time, and never hangs out; very predictable. He is also a great provider and father.

"Bad boys ain't no good. Good guys ain't no fun."
- Mary J. Blige, Mr. Wrong

However, he is mentally, physically, and spiritually boring. Thus, he can't carry on an intelligent conversation, and he is sexually complacent - no excitement, no stimulation. However, you don't want to leave him because he's genuinely a *Nice Guy* and you think it's unfair for your children not to see their father daily. Thus, you seek out a person that can satisfy your void of boredom, which is the *Side Piece*.

"I always knew when he wanted to have sex. He had the same routine. He would light the fireplace, light some candles, dim the lights, and play the same Luther Vandross album. We

have sex in the same position, which is missionary. After about 12 minutes he climaxes and then rolls over and goes to sleep. I'm over it."
- Ms. Parker

Variety

You married the man of your dreams, but let's keep it real, you have always functioned like a guy. Not in a masculine way, because you are quite feminine. I'm talking about having a male's mentality, as far as promiscuity. You love your husband and family, and you don't have any marital issues. However, you do enjoy the occasional outside penis, for recreational purposes only. It's not often, just when you attend your college homecoming and a few business conferences throughout the year. If your husband found out, he would be devastated. If you caught him cheating on you, you would ask for a divorce. You understand it's hypocritical, but you just like a little variety every now and then.

"I wasn't having any issues in my Marriage and I had never cheated, but it was something about this one particular guy. When I first saw him I was like, 'who is this Zulu Warrior of a man?' I knew I was going to fuck him."
- Natasha

"The One"

You were unsuccessful in your quest to marry the guy you really wanted to marry because he was not ready, so you decided to marry someone else. Your husband is a great guy, but the guy you really wanted to marry was and still is "The One." He is the barometer you use when evaluating other men you encounter, including your husband. You still remain friends with him to this day. You don't see or talk to him often, but when you speak or see each other, you pick up right where you left off. He will always have a special place in your heart and he can always get it no matter who you are with. You don't consider being with him as cheating because you are still in love with him. The rules do not apply to "The One." Nonetheless, you are still conflicted about him from time to time.

> *"Listen, he was my first. You were my second. I'm not having sex with anyone else. I'm either going to marry you or him. I would prefer to marry you. It's your choice. Let me know something soon."*
> *- Shelby*

How do many of these situations come to be if you don't interact or communicate with other men out of respect for your *Marriage*? Even if you wanted to have a *Side Piece*, you have no idea of how to get one. In rare cases, a small percentage of

women will find a complete stranger to avoid having an emotional attachment. She will probably discover this random guy at a night club or on a girl's trip to the Caribbean. Some women will just contact a guy from a recent encounter or previous relationship. This process is called "recycling the penis." Their rationale is they don't want their "body count" to increase because they have always prided themselves on being able to count all the people they had sex with on one hand. They're also familiar with the recent guy. If not the recent guy, it may be the high school or college sweetheart or a man recommended by a trusted friend that has her own *Side Piece*. Others will link up with a guy they encounter in their social, work, or business environment, such as a co-worker, supervisor, or their personal trainer.

> *"I have a girlfriend that meets her Side Piece at business conferences, once or twice a year. Out-of-state of course. I remember one time, she created a fake business conference. She even created a PowerPoint presentation, flyers, and an itinerary for an event that didn't even exist. She's good! Her husband is so clueless. He was probably thinking about how much pussy he was going to get while she was gone."*
> *- Misty*

Of course, it probably won't happen immediately. If and when it does, it will only be when there is a window of

opportunity. These windows can be ajar for an infinite amount of time or just for a nanosecond. If the right person appears at the right time, he will be inside that window.

> *"Men really think that women don't have time to cheat because they always have the kids (cock-blockers) with them. Plus, they have to take them to their extracurricular activities, such as soccer practice. This way of thinking is a mistake. Let me tell you why. Soccer practice starts at 6:30 P.M. and lasts approximately two hours. The wife is able to drop the child off at 6:15 P.M. because the coach always arrives early. Her Side Piece lives approximately 15 minutes away from the soccer field. She reaches her destination at 6:30 P.M. and takes her clothes off as she walks through the door. She has time to give him fellatio, have multiple orgasms, pillow talk, take a quick hoe bath (wash up in the sink), and still have time to get back to the soccer field to pick up her kid by 8:15 P.M. Finally, she gets home and has enough time and energy to cook dinner and check homework."*
>
> *- Osei*

Just because you're married, that does not mean you are blind. Therefore, you notice a guy at your job that is attractive, charismatic, articulate, has an athletic build, and always smells really good. However, you never give it a second thought

because you are married. Your encounters consist of, "Hello!" "How are you doing?" "Have a nice day." and "See you tomorrow." As your *Marriage* starts to deteriorate, those conversations morph into, "Would you like to go to lunch?" "Do you mind if I give you a call?" and "What are you doing this weekend?" By the way, this guy always notices the little things that your husband never notices, like a new haircut, new fragrance, and weight loss after the baby.

> *"A sign that your significant other is possibly cheating on you is when they suddenly make love to you in a way that's outside of their character; doing moves you've never seen before."*
> *- Gladys*

It starts off very innocently. A phone call here or there, lunch every once in a while, but no sex, just stimulating conversation. Conversations that consist of intimate information, politics, education, travel, and an array of other topics that you never discuss with your other half. You love the fact that you're always learning something new from each encounter. Even at this point, you are still trying to do the right thing.

In an attempt to salvage your *Marriage*, you try to replicate your new relationship. You go home and try to get your husband to adopt some of the ideas and behaviors you

learned from the other guy to no avail, because he has no interest. He is fine with the way things are and he does not see any problems. Unknowingly, he is complicit in you cheating on him. Before you know it, you have a husband and a *Side Piece*, which you consider your boyfriend that you're emotionally attached to. However, unlike the female *Side Piece*, the male *Side Piece* is content with his position and in most cases, doesn't want you to leave your husband.

Catching feelings for your *Side Piece* may pose a problem. Here's why. Male *Side Pieces* generally understand their position and don't want anything to change because it accommodates their single lifestyle. They get all the benefits (sex, fellatio, quality time…) of a relationship and none of the unwanted aspects (accountability, obligation, questioning, rehashing conversations, arguments, nagging…) of actually having to be in one. Additionally, he only trusts you to a certain extent because he sees you cheating on your husband.

"Please don't leave your husband for me. I would never be in a real relationship with you because you are a cheater. You must be crazy!"
- Roberto

I know, I know…you told him, "My husband and I are just roommates." "We sleep in separate rooms." "He won't sign the divorce papers." "We're only together for the kids." and

"We don't have sex anymore." Guess what? That's what all married people say to their *Side Pieces*, male and female. Sometimes they are telling the truth, other times they are not. There is no way for your *Side Piece* to really know, because you and your spouse are the only ones that really know what's going down in your household.

"If she cheats on him to be with you, she has the propensity to cheat on you with someone else. You can't trust her."
- Bobby L. Rosemond

As a "rule of thumb," if you want to start a new relationship, you should completely end the old relationship first. Completely! Look at the situation like baking a cake. Let's say you baked a Red Velvet Cake, but now you want to make a Ghanaian Chocolate Cake. If you intend on using the same bowl to mix the ingredients for the Ghanaian Chocolate Cake you used for the Red Velvet Cake, what must you do first? Precisely, you must clean your bowl thoroughly. If not, whenever you taste a slice of your new Ghanaian Chocolate Cake you may taste remnants of the old Red Velvet Cake.

"Never let your past interfere with your future."
- Kelly

Remember, if fidelity is your top priority, marry someone that you are compatible with. Don't go after men that you know

will never be a one-woman man. I know, I know... those are the guys with the edge, charisma, presence, swagger, and are the most confident, which is what draws a plethora of women to them. Also, don't pursue men that are incapable of meeting most of your needs. You should figure out what's most important to you. Do you want extraordinary and possibly unfaithful; or ordinary and monogamous? Now, don't get me wrong, I am not saying that there is not a man out there that possesses the elements of extraordinary and monogamous; however, I will say, in my opinion, it is quite rare. If that is in fact what you want, don't settle, because entering a *Marriage* with someone should not be taken lightly.

CAKE

MARRIAGE

How does the idea of *Marriage* sound to you right now? Do you think you really want to get married? Why do you want to get married? What does *Marriage* mean to you? Do you think your idea of *Marriage* is aligned with the individuals you encounter that may be a potential candidate for *Marriage*? What might be the implications if your *Marriage* ideals are not aligned?

Who you marry and who you procreate with may be two of the most important decisions you will ever make. Yet, even in light of the high divorce rate in America, the average couple doesn't seem to take the institution of *Marriage* seriously. There are individuals that research and do their due diligence when applying to a college, purchasing a car, buying a house, traveling to another country, and many other important decisions; yet who they marry doesn't seem to garner the same

scrutiny. Let that sink in for a moment. When you are going through the process of vetting an individual you think you want to spend the rest of your life with, you must make sure that your idea of *Marriage* is aligned with theirs. There may be distinct differences in an individual's ideologies as it relates to *Marriage*, whether it's religious, cultural, or innate.

Common mating or reproductively motivated systems include monogamy, polygamy, polygyny (Harem), polyandry, and polygynandry. Monogamy is the practice of being with one person at a time. Polygamy is the practice of having more than one husband or wife at a time. Polygyny, polyandry, and polygynandry are all variations of polygamy that will be discussed further. Religion and culture seemingly draw their concept of *Marriage* or unions from the aforementioned systems.

The concept of *Marriage*, or the union of individuals, predates recorded written history. Today, Western culture views *Marriage* as a monogamous bond between two individuals that is predicated on love and companionship. Historically, that was not necessarily the case. Depending on religion, culture, and time period, *Marriage* was a way of expanding the family labor force, gaining in-laws, and making alliances, with many *Marriages* being brokered and arranged by the elders. Love was not a part of the equation. Even though

monogamy may seem to be the core of how *Marriage* is qualified today, polygamy was quite prevalent throughout history and presently in various parts of the world.

> *"Ain't nothing natural about monogamy. God did not intend for us to be with just one person. If he had, he wouldn't have given us all these sperm. These bitches would not outnumber us the way that they do. Y'all know as well as I do, ain't nothing better than some pussy, except some new pussy."*
> *- Quentin, The Best Man*

Monogamy

Traditionally, Western matrimony is between a man and a woman, which is qualified as a monogamous relationship. Monogamy became the guiding principle for Western *Marriages* sometime between the sixth and the ninth century. Additionally, for more than 2,500 years, the Western legal tradition has qualified lawful *Marriage* as the union of one man and one woman, with the capacity, freedom, and fitness to marry each other. This was the most prevalent teaching of first millennium European Jews and Christians, common law and civil law jurists, Romans and Greeks, Modern Enlightenment philosophers and liberals, medieval Catholics, and early modern Protestants. Currently, the preferred choice of *Marriage* for Western societies is also monogamy. However,

monogamy is not the preferred choice of all societies. Some societies prefer plural *Marriages* or polygamy.

Polygamy

Polygamy consists of *Marriage* between multiple partners, and can fall under a broader category of polyamory. On a global scale, polygamy is a very common practice that is normal and accepted. According to the <u>Ethnographic Atlas Codebook</u> – derived from George P. Murdock's <u>Ethnographic Atlas,</u> of 1,231 noted societies, 186 were identified as monogamous, 453 practiced occasional polygamy, 588 had more frequent polygamy, and four had polyandry. These societies' marital composition was recorded from 1960-1980.

"Some people are in polygamous relationships and they're the only one that don't know."
- Samantha

As an umbrella term, polygamy is a moniker used to describe various non-monogamous interactions. The three mating systems that fall under the polygamous umbrella are polyandry, polygyny, and polygynandry. To be more specific, when a woman is married to multiple men it is called polyandry; when a man has more than one wife, the relationship is qualified as polygyny; and when a family consists of multiple husbands and wives, this situation is considered a polygynandry arrangement.

MARRIAGE

"I've always felt that monogamy was unnatural. I don't feel I should have to have only one sexual partner for the entirety of my life. I like variety. Subsequently, I've always dated men that had similar sentiments. Presently, I've been married to my husband for six years, and my husband and I have participated in the lifestyle (swinging, orgies, threesomes...) since we met. We are currently entertaining the idea of marrying another couple. I'm so excited!"

- Noni

Arguments

Proponents for both lifestyles have very strong opinions. Believers in monogamy feel that enduring an exclusive monogamous *Marriage* is the most optimal way to ensure joint paternal investment in children and paternal certainty. Additionally, monogamous unions supposedly guarantee equal treatment between sexes as it relates to respect and dignity. These types of *Marriages* also ensure that husbands and wives, as well as parents and children, provide each other with mutual protection, edification and support for a lifetime, contingent on changes in an individual's needs at different stages in the life cycle.

Polygamy, on the other hand, has not only been completely condemned by Western culture, it has been

criminalized. The most common argument for the condemnation of polygamy was that it was unfair, unjust, and unnatural to wives and children, as a violation of their fundamental rights in modern parlance. Recent Western writers have expressed that polygamy was a threat to political stability, good citizenship, and social order. Additional literature states that it could even be an impediment to the advancement of civilizations toward democratic government, equality, and liberty.

> *"I don't see why some people feel the need to be with multiple people. I think one person should be sufficient."*
> *- Karen*

Of course, the views of polygamists are entirely different than their monogamous counterparts. Polygamists feel that plural *Marriage* is about building and maintaining strong families and communities, not sex. Furthermore, polygamists believe that the reasons or functions of plural unions include: addressing the problem of a surplus of women in a particular community; increased probability of children, specifically when a wife is barren or gives birth to a female child; and increasing the labor supply within a family kinship.

With that being said, not all men that are permitted to have multiple wives actually choose to have a plural *Marriage*. Some of these individuals are content with living a

monogamous life with one wife. Thus, polygamists don't necessarily have an issue or argument against monogamy, but more so an argument as it relates to the hypocrisy of Western societies that condemn polygamy as a deviant lifestyle. Yet, many monogamists practice a variation of polygamy covertly.

> *"Western men are such hypocrites. They condemn people that believe in and practice polygamy, yet they marry one women and have mistresses. All my wives know about each other. There are no secrets."*
> *-Amadou*

The rebuttal further explains that many individuals in these societies that claim to be monogamous choose to indulge in extra-marital affairs, threesomes, open *Marriages*, and other alternative lifestyles, such as swinging (swapping spouses). It seems that both worlds of polygamy and monogamy share similar traits, the only difference seems to be not giving full disclosure of relationships. It makes you wonder, are humans innately monogamous or polygamous? Have humans been socialized to think a certain way? Polygamists would argue that as human animals, monogamy is not natural, especially for men - just look at the animal kingdom.

Animal Kingdom

Yes, homo sapiens or humans are animals, a very intelligent *Species* of animals, but nonetheless, animals;

mammals in particular. Compared to other animals, humans differ by having formal *Marriages*. However, they are quite similar as it relates to their mating systems, as well as other similarities.

The mating system of true monogamy is almost non-existent in the animal kingdom. True monogamy consists of social, sexual, and genetic monogamy. Social monogamy refers to the male and female's exclusive social living arrangement. For humans, social monogamy is *Marriage*. Sexual monogamy is qualified as an exclusive sexual relationship between a male and a female based on observations of sexual interactions. Lastly, genetic monogamy is the verification of a male-female pairing, procreating exclusively with each other utilizing the analyses of DNA. DNA or Deoxyribonucleic is an acid molecule that contains the instructions an organism needs to develop, live, and reproduce, that is passed from parent to child.

In the 1990s, scientists believed that 90% of the bird *Species* were truly monogamous. This was the highest rate of true monogamy amongst all animals. Conversely, just three to five percent of all mammal *Species* were thought to be monogamous. Any form of monogamy among fish, reptiles, and amphibians was quite rare. This was before the discovery of DNA fingerprinting.

DNA fingerprinting is the equivalent of paternity tests used in the courts to verify the paternity of human children. In light of the new technology, scientists not only discovered that monogamy was rarer than previously believed, they are also reluctant to classify any *Species* as truly monogamous until it has undergone rigorous DNA fingerprinting. DNA fingerprinting examines blood samples of offspring to establish paternity. The *Species* that were thought to be monogamous were only socially monogamous, but sexually or genetically polygamous. This form of monogamy is qualified as pair bonding between male and female. Meaning male and female mate with each other, spend time together, and raise offspring together. However, they may occasionally mate outside their pair bond. Such outside mating is defined as "extra pair copulations."

> *"When you're used to dealing with a multitude of people, it's more of a challenge to be with just one person. When you're not used to getting any action at all, being with one person in a monogamous Marriage is much easier."*
> *- Shaka*

I know what you're thinking, human-beings are not like other animals. People are supposed to have more self-control, right? Depending on what type of person you encounter, they may or may not agree with you. That's why it's imperative to

know who and what you're dealing with. Undoubtedly, there are many similarities between humans and other *Species* in the animal kingdom as it relates to common mating systems. However, unlike humans, animals can easily distinguish one *Species* from the other, so they never make the mistake of mating with an animal that is different because within their *Species*, they all look alike.

Humans must put forth more of an effort to make sure that if they are a gazelle, they don't hitch their wagon to a cheetah, figuratively speaking. The consequences of these misguided unions could be catastrophic. As a human, once you identify a mating system that is appropriate for you, you must also self-reflect and do your research, to ultimately understand and identify what *Species* you are. Once you know yourself, you can better determine what you are looking for and who you are most compatible with.

> *"Losing yourself in hopes of pleasing somebody else is the hardest part of Marriage."*
> *- Marcellus*

JELLY BEANS

SPECIES

The animal kingdom consists of a myriad of *Species*. Within each major category of *Species*, there are specific characteristics that distinguish one *Species* from the other. These characteristics include types of reproduction, livable climates, types of foods eaten, and where they are in the food chain. There are also certain rules in the animal kingdom that are impossible to break, and certain rubicons that are impossible to cross, giving it a certain order.

One of those rules is that you can only mate within your *Species*, for the most part. For instance, if you were an alligator relaxing in the river delta and you really admired the appearance of a giraffe nearby; would you desire to mate with them? Is it possible? Of course not, because you are an alligator and your only option is to mate with another alligator. If you were an animal that only ate plants, could you mate with a lion?

Absolutely not. As a natural predator, the lion would probably devour you on the spot. There is no way around it. Animals naturally knowing what they are and who they can mate with is a luxury. For human animals, it's not that easy. Unfortunately, the spots, stripes, and scales are not as apparent.

As previously stated, DNA is an acid molecule that contains the instructions an organism needs to develop, live, and reproduce. These instructions are found inside every cell. There are certain things coded in one's DNA that are innate. For example, it is coded in the DNA of a wolf to attack and devour a sheep if they cross paths. This is their undisputed nature.

For the purpose of this body of work, DNA will be qualified as the various elements and characteristics that contribute to or identify who or what a person is (e. g., values, personality, and character). In addition to a person's DNA, who you're raised by, life experiences, levels of education, and various types of life exposure, also contribute to one's *Species.*

One of the many philosophies which guide my life as it relates to relationships is that you attract what you are, what you relate to, or what complements you. Whether it's a romantic or platonic relationship, people tend to be drawn to individuals with similar interests, backgrounds, ideologies, levels of ambition, education, and overall energy. The problem

is some people don't know what or who they are. Therefore, it's challenging for them to find a compatible consort. I've delineated a few categories you may be able to identify with. I will provide you with overall descriptions and describe the dichotomy of these characteristics between the sexes. Of course, there are obvious and broad descriptions of various types of people such as extrovert, introvert, giving, and selfish. These examples will be more specific. Hopefully you can determine your *Species* in order to find a compatible mate.

Independent Thinker

The *Independent Thinker* views life through their Third Eye. The Third Eye is known as the Eye of Horus, which is the Kemetic symbol for royalty, power, good health, and protection. The Third Eye (also known as the inner eye) is an esoteric and mystical concept referring to a projected invisible eye which provides perception beyond conventional sight. A person that has tapped into their Third Eye looks at life differently than the average person.

"You can't just pee in my glass and say its lemonade."
- Nia

There are various names for people that have discovered their Third Eye. One of the more common names is "conscious" or *Independent Thinker*. Some would say they're all brain (cerebral), not only highly intellectual, but also sexually stimulated by intellect (sapiosexual). Thus, these individuals are always looking for the rhyme and reason in all situations and are not satisfied unless a definitive explanation is surmised. Explanation for them is unearthed through infinite research, being an avid reader of different types of literature, having conversations with an array of individuals, travel, and/or life experiences overall.

> *"I'm a true sapiosexual. I need someone that will give me mental orgasms."*
> *- Penelope*
> *sāpēō'sekSH(oō)əl/: a person who finds intelligence sexually attractive or arousing.*

Independent Thinkers are constantly thinking, even in their sleep. They are very analytical and pensive, viewing life through a logical prism. They don't make moves haphazardly, they are very methodical. Some people may even perceive them to be robots or some kind of cyborg. *Independent Thinkers* will constantly stimulate you mentally and always teach you something new. As an "out of the box" thinker, do not expect him or her to function in ordinary ways. If you choose the person that uses all three eyes, be prepared to keep up, mentally, spiritually, and physically, or you will be left behind. In the game of life, they are playing chess not checkers, which means they are thinking of multiple moves beyond their current

circumstances. They are also unapologetically different than the majority of the world.

> "The Matrix is everywhere. It is all around us. Even now, in this very room. You can see it when you look out your window or when you turn on your television. You can feel it when you go to work, when you go to church, when you pay your taxes. It is the world that has been pulled over your eyes to blind you from the truth. The truth that you are a slave, Neo. Like everyone else you were born into bondage, born into a prison that you cannot smell or taste or touch. A prison for your mind. Unfortunately, no one can be told what The Matrix is. You have to see it for yourself. This is your last chance. After this, there is no turning back. You take the blue pill. The story ends. You wake up in your bed and believe...whatever you want to believe. You take the red pill. You stay in Wonderland and I show you how deep the rabbit hole goes. Remember, all I'm offering is the truth. Nothing more."
>
> ~ Morpheus, The Matrix

Sheep

Have you ever heard the phrase, "ignorance is bliss?" Many people live in this state of mind because it's easy. Individuals that are familiar with the movie, *The Matrix*, would say that these people live in *The Matrix*. *The Matrix* is a movie about making the choice to live in a world that is a façade; or embracing reality no matter how harsh the truth. Most individuals you encounter live in *The Matrix* and are okay with not knowing certain things because it's less responsibility. I liken it to the life of a *Sheep*.

Sheep follow blindly almost never questioning anything or anybody. They are a follower of many different groups. Typically, they follow a particular religion, have favorite sports teams, belong to a particular political party, and overall think and follow in accordance with their ethnicity, sex, religion, and/or the geographical location in which they were born. *Sheep* find it very challenging to leave the herd and think "outside of the box." For them ignorance is truly bliss.

"People want to latch on to something that makes them feel good about themselves."
- Michael Wilbon

Ballers

Ballers use their status, wealth, and material possessions as their mouthpiece. When you meet them initially, that's the focus of their entire conversation. They're constantly asking you:

"What can I purchase for you?"

"Can I take you out to eat or for a drink?"

"Can I take you on a trip?"

"Do you need me to pay some of your bills......?"

"Law 40: Despise the Free Lunch: What is offered for free is dangerous – it usually involves either a trick or hidden obligation. What has worth is worth paying for. By paying your own way you stay clear of gratitude, guilt, and deceit."
- Robert Greene, The 48 Laws of Power

In essence, they are asking you, "How much is it going to cost for us to have sex?" Some women see it as the guy treating her like she's special. The *Baller* qualifies it as just another conquest and he will move on to the next one when he's done. *Ballers* are very generous but also very controlling. As long as you adhere to their program, everything will remain copacetic. However, if you get out-of-pocket, you will be dismissed and replaced.

"A woman usually believes that when a man buys her nice things, it means he really cares about her. That's not necessarily true. It could mean he has the money and resources to buy things for multiple women. He could be trying to buy her off. She should be very careful, gifts may give her a false sense of reality."
- Jayesh

Boss

Have you ever heard a woman say, "I want a man like my grandfather?" "I'm old-fashioned." or "I need a real man that is

willing to pay for everything (e.g., mortgage, car notes, insurance, travel, and activities)." Women, be very careful about what you ask for. Understand, when you say you want a man like your grandfather, be careful because you may not necessarily know everything about your grandfather. My mother once told me if her grandfather said, "I'll be back later," as he walked out the house, that was a courtesy. I have heard similar sentiments echoed from many people that grew up in the same era. This way of thinking was and still is, "paying the cost to be the *Boss*."

This type of man has no problem with paying for everything, because he understands that the person that is financing everything, is the person that possess the power and that's how he likes it. Both people benefit, right? The woman has the choice of working or not working, have her dream wedding, buy anything she desires, live in her dream home, go on all-inclusive trips, and never have to spend one dime of her personal money. The man on the other hand gets to control the entire program (e.g., finances, children, and the wife) because he gladly pays the cost to be the *Boss*. If the couple has two children, the wife is basically the third child. This trait is generally not part of a women's innate identity or DNA. Some women seek to be the *Boss*, but not often. However, when it does happen, her modus operandi is the same or similar.

Sugar Daddy

Historically, a *Sugar Daddy* is known as an older man that desires to share company with women that are significantly younger and they don't mind spending money on them. A *Sugar Daddy* is similar to a *Boss*, but nicer and has less expectations. *Sugar Daddies* are usually older and have lived a full life. Some have made a fortune as successful entrepreneurs. Others have merely been hard workers all their life and are collecting multiple retirement, disability, and/or social security checks. They have been married and divorced a number of times or widowed and all their children are grown, with their own families.

Sugar Daddies are mainly interested in companionship. With the discovery of male enhancement medication, sex may or may not be involved, depending on his health. They prefer a young tender (younger woman) they can go out in public with as their show piece. They don't mind taking a young lady on shopping sprees, all-expense paid vacations, and paying for extravagant dinners. Ultimately, they just want someone to put a smile on their face from time to time as they live out their "Golden Years."

Cougar

A *Cougar*, in contrast with a *Sugar Daddy*, is a woman that prefers the company of a younger man. Now a *Cougar* may or may not have been married and had children. Unlike the *Sugar Daddy*, sex is always part of the equation. The *Cougar* is always ready. She could have always been a hardworking, driven, career oriented woman that never married. On the other hand, she could be a divorcee or a widow that's living off her husband's retirement, alimony, life insurance, and/or social security income. Now that she is older and past her child bearing years, "the *Ring*" is not necessarily all that important. However, she does get lonely from time to time and enjoys the occasional company of a young virile man.

Pushover

By definition, a *Pushover* is a person who is easy to overcome or influence and doesn't mind compromising. In many cases *Pushovers* are perceived to be weak and lack self-confidence. They have a tendency to want to please everyone, neglect themselves, and they are "loyal to a fault." Pay attention to the following examples.

Nice Guy

Male *Pushovers* are considered to be the *Nice Guys*. Being the *Nice Guy* is not necessarily a good thing. Women say they want a *Nice Guy*, but from my personal experience and life observations, that is not always true. I know, I know... you are saying, "Why wouldn't a woman want a *Nice Guy*?" Granted, a *Nice Guy* is going to get up and go to work every day and

come home at the same time. He will ensure that the bills are paid, help take care of the kids, do yard work, and help with household chores. Anytime you want to purchase something or do something, he will simply say, "yes" or "anything you want dear." Also, the extent of his extracurricular activities are watching the game and going bowling on Thursday night. The *Nice Guy* will suffice only temporarily, until the female feels her life is boring and she realizes that the man she married is boring, uneventful, and does not want to change. At least he will be faithful, right? Not necessarily. There are no guarantees.

"I used to be the Nice Guy, until it came back to bite me. One day I was taking a young lady friend of mine out to eat. As we were leaving my house, she stated that she couldn't find her cell phone. I said I would call her phone so that she could listen for the ring to retrieve it. When I called the phone, I heard it between the huge cushions on my sofa. Once I retrieved the phone, it was still ringing from my call. As I picked it up, I noticed the screen. She had my number saved in her phone as 'Free Food.' I was stunned and hurt. I didn't say anything. I carried on as if everything was fine. Yes, we still went to dinner. When the check came, I instructed the waiter to split the check. She exclaimed she didn't have any money. I paid for my meal, shot her the peace sign and left her in the restaurant. Since then, I've only

dated foreign women. Needless to say, I truly understand the old adage, 'Nice Guys finish last.'"
- Brad

Good Girl

The exact same characteristics of a *Nice Guy* that are prevalent in the female are perceived somewhat differently. This female is deemed a *Good Girl*. She's a great wife, mother, and homemaker. She hasn't been with a plethora of men, which is a great thing, because most men do not want to marry a promiscuous woman. Also, unlike the *Nice Guy*, the *Good Girl* is open to change and trying new things, because women don't mind learning from men. In many cases they crave mental stimulation.

Alphas

Alphas have a Type A personality. Typically, people with Type A personalities are ambitious, highly driven and head strong. They may have a high level of confidence that could be misconstrued as arrogance. *Alphas* generally march to the beat of their own drum and they run their world by their own set of rules. They consider themselves to be at the top of the food chain and could really care less about what most people think about them.

SPECIES

Alpha Male

Typically, being an *Alpha Male* with a Type A personality is perceived as a very positive characteristic for a man to possess. These men are born leaders that typically become entrepreneurs, leaders of nations, politicians, CEO's, college presidents, and religious leaders. However, in a relationship these men can be perceived as controlling, selfish, insensitive, and a dictator. However, the negative perceived characteristics of a male with a Type A personality won't prevent him from getting married anytime he chooses to whomever he chooses. The reality for the *Independent Woman* is quite different.

Independent Woman

An *Alpha Female* with a Type A personality can be considered a blessing and a curse. A term that has been coined to describe this female character trait is, *Independent Woman* or "head strong woman." This woman has been driven to be successful her whole life. While building her career, being tied down by any man was the last thing on her mind. She is successful in every area of her life except for relationships. She has at least three degrees, possibly her own business, pays her own bills, purchased her first home by the age of 28, has a luxury car, and a small dog that she treats like her child. She has always had to take care of everything, whether that is maintaining her yard, cleaning the gutters, or getting

maintenance on her car. She either handles it herself or finds someone to do it. As a result, she develops a "proverbial penis" and she LOVES it. I call this the *Oprah Effect*. However, what's the one thing that's missing? Correct... a husband and children. Why is that you ask?

> *"I'm independent by force, not by choice. I'm tired of watering myself down to make insecure men feel strong."*
> *- Alisha*

Here is the problem that an *Independent Woman* will face if she refuses to be malleable. Pay close attention! She claims she wants a man that is as equally, or more focused and driven than her, which would be the *Alpha Male*. However, the *Alpha Male,* who is as equally driven as her, will be perceived as a dictator and controlling, because she is used to running the show and controlling her world. She's used to being a leader. She believes being submissive is an antiquated concept and that there should be two head coaches in a household versus a head coach and an assistant coach. She refuses to relinquish her "proverbial penis" and unfortunately with the *Alpha Male*, that's not going to work. No heterosexual man wants to be with a woman that acts like a man. Her consolation prize is the *Nice Guy*.

SPECIES

"You don't need a man, you are a man."
- Antonio

The *Nice Guy* definitely can't satisfy her, because while having a man that allows her to do whatever she wants is a novel idea, it would be short lived because no woman wants a man that will let her run over him. It may seem to be a great situation initially, however, she will eventually realize that her penis is bigger than his, figuratively speaking, and inevitably emasculate this man. That's not going to work, because again, no woman innately wants to lead a man.

Consequently, even though she may procreate, this woman will have a series of failed *Marriages*/relationships, become a *Cougar*, be alone, or find a girlfriend. And yes, I am saying become a lesbian. If you don't believe me, assess the successful, driven, *Independent Women* you know in your personal everyday life, that has decided not to relinquish some of their independence (proverbial penis) for a quality man. Also, look at women (Oprah Winfrey, Madonna, Mariah Carey, Jennifer Lopez, Rosie O'Donnell, Barbara Walters, Halle Berry, Ellen DeGeneres, Elizabeth Taylor...) that are highly successful in the world of entertainment, business, media, Hollywood, and overall pop culture. Investigate for your own edification.

Super Freak

Rick James was a Rhythm & Blues singer that was very popular in the 70s and 80s. One of his most renowned songs was *Super Freak*. Not only was *Super Freak* the name of one of his most popular songs, he was also known as a *Super Freak* (promiscuous) as well. His alternative sexual exploits were not a secret and are well documented. He is not alone. There is a segment of society that really loves sex, all types of sex. The academic terms for these individuals are satyriasis for men and nymphomaniac for women. Colloquial terms consist of freaks, hoes, cuddy, T.H.O.T. (That Hoe Over There), and slut. Most of the aforementioned terms are used to describe promiscuous women. They can be used to describe men as well. However, men generally don't care. They tend to wear these labels as badges of honor. Only a few women possess similar sentiments.

Nevertheless, *Super Freaks* are not monolithic in their activities. The main similarity is that they really love sex and are willing to explore different things, sexually. With that being said, *Super Freaks* can be many different things. There are those that enjoy watching sexual acts known as voyeurs and others that enjoy being watched while they are engaging in sexual acts, known as exhibitionists. Others participate in alternative lifestyles that involve threesomes, swinging, and orgies. For some, this may be a passing phase, for others it's a lifestyle.

Double Agent

For the purpose of describing a *Double Agent*, we will look at sexuality through three lenses. Yes, I know, you probably already have an awareness of various sexual orientations. However, I would like to introduce a new category. The most common type of sexual orientation is heterosexuality. Heterosexuals prefer to partner with individuals of the opposite sex. On the opposite end of the spectrum is homosexuality. Homosexuals prefer to link up with individuals of the same sex. Then there are individuals that function in the middle of the road, who are bisexual. Bisexuals prefer both sexes. Individuals that identify with one of the aforementioned areas of sexuality usually have no problem with being open about what or who they desire. When you come in contact with these individuals, their sexual orientation is not covert. They are very open and proud of their lifestyle. *Double Agents* are not as easy to identify.

Double Agents, whether male or female, have a desire for both sexes. However, it's a lifestyle they don't necessarily want everyone to know about. Also, the realities and perception of the male and female *Double Agent* are vastly different. Not right or wrong, just different.

"I will never cheat on you with another man. However, on occasion I will have sex with a woman, for recreation purposes only. From time to time, I will let you join us."
- Diana

First, let's look at the female *Double Agent*. The female *Double Agent*, also known as a *Pillow Princess* presents herself as heterosexual and feminine. She has no desire to be in a committed long-term relationship with a woman; that position is designated for a man - the future father of her children. However, she does yearn for the soft, feminine touch of a female every now and then for recreational purposes only. She does not want to cuddle, go on dates or do anything romantic with other females. Female *Double Agents* basically treat women like married men treat their mistresses and/or *Side Pieces*. They do not consider themselves gay or bisexual. Even though female *Double Agents* are not completely open about their alternative lifestyle, they are somewhat comfortable if select individuals are aware of their occasional guilty pleasure.

"I feel that most women are two drinks away from entertaining or engaging in a bisexual or homosexual experience."
- Carlos

The male *Double Agent* has similar characteristics, however social acceptance is diametrically different. The male

Double Agent also characterizes himself as heterosexual and has a seemingly masculine appearance. He has no desire to date, have a relationship, or raise children with another man. He definitely wants to partner and live his life with a female. However, from time to time he likes to engage sexually with another man. Just like the female *Double Agent*, the male *Double Agent* does not consider himself gay or bisexual. However, the male *Double Agent* absolutely does not want anyone to know about his little secret. This lifestyle is considered being on the "Down Low" and was depicted in the movie *Broke Back Mountain.*

> *"I believe that you can love anyone. I've had relationships with women, I've had relationships with men. I don't think you should be judged based on who you find attractive. Especially guys - gay men, they really have it hard sometimes."*
> *- Amber Rose*

Female *Double Agents* tend to be more open about their alternative lifestyle because overall female bisexuality and homosexuality seems to be more socially tolerable. Additionally, some of their male counterparts even welcome the idea, hoping for a possible threesome. Male *Double Agents* are not as open. Unlike the male's acceptance of a female's occasional desire for women, women do not feel the same way.

They are absolutely, unequivocally opposed to the idea. Yes, it's a *Double Standard*.

Religious Fanatic

You have people that practice or subscribe to a particular religion and utilize it as a tool for guidance in various areas of their life. At the same time, these individuals respect and coexist with other individuals that choose to practice other belief systems and religions without judgment, in harmony. Then you have other individuals that view the concept of religion entirely different, in a more dogmatic manner. I qualify these individuals as *Religious Fanatics*.

"Whomever I marry, we have to be equally yoked."
- Christina

Him: "From your understanding, what is a yoke?"

Her: "The yolk of an egg, right?"

Him: "(Laughing) Are you serious?"

Her: "Yes!"

Him: "No, I didn't say yolk, y - o - l - k. I said yoke, y - o - k - e. How are you a preacher's kid that's always pushing religion on others and you don't know what the hell you're talking about most of the time? You are just regurgitating what you heard from someone else."

Her: "I never thought about it like that. Can you please finish explaining?"

Him: "A yoke is a wooden crosspiece that is fastened to the necks of two animals, such as a mule or oxen. The animals are responsible for pulling a plow to sow seeds or a cart for transportation. If the animals are not equal in stature, the plow or cart will be pulled unevenly. Similar to a relationship. When two people are not equal in various fundamental areas of their lives and still choose to embark on a relationship, it may be a bumpy ride."

Her: "Wow that makes sense. I didn't know."

Him: "Now you know. You must learn to research things for yourself. Don't just follow blindly, be an Independent Thinker, not a Sheep."

Religion is an organized system of rituals, ceremonies, beliefs, and rules used to worship a god or group of gods, created by man. A fanatic is someone filled with single-minded and extreme enthusiasm for an extreme political or religious cause. *Religious Fanatics* believe their religion or belief system is the supreme religion. All other religions and belief systems are wrong. Furthermore, as a result of people choosing to practice the "wrong" religion, they are going to suffer grave consequences in the afterlife. Depending on the religion and the person, this concept may take on different forms. Let's look at some examples:

- Whenever you have a conversation with this person, it's chock-full of scriptures from a religious book or quotes from a particular deity, dead or alive.
- The majority of their time is spent in a religious building.
- They consistently give a portion of their earnings to a religious institution.
- If someone says something that conflicts with their belief, they become defensive.
- Whenever the idea of learning about another religion arises, they refuse to listen, because they feel no need to learn anything new. In their mind, any new information would be averse to how they feel or what they believe.

"Some people over analyze things. Too much knowledge can be bad for you. All I need to know about life is in this book."
- Ms. Jenkins

The aforementioned examples are some common indicators, but not the only indicators of a *Religious Fanatic*. Additionally, this individual will want you to practice and function in the same or similar fashion. This may include visiting a worship center on a certain day, wearing certain clothes, celebrating certain holidays, or raising children in a

certain fashion that's aligned with the religion they practice. There is no deviation from what they believe in. They usually don't have a problem dating or marrying as it relates to religion, because they typically deal with individuals exclusive to their community. This only becomes a problem when *Religious Fanatics* attempt to foster a relationship with someone that thinks outside of their religious scope.

Spiritual Being

Some people believe religion and spirituality are synonymous. Others believe they are completely different. Spirituality is a broad concept with room for a variety of viewpoints. Basically, it encompasses a sense of connection to something greater and typically involves a concept of searching for the meaning of life. Spirituality spawns questions such as: "Why are we here?" and "What is our purpose?"

The *Spiritual Being* may feel that religion divides people as a whole. They are often characterized, by religious people, as atheists. Atheists are individuals that don't believe in a higher power. People that are spiritual are quite the contrary. *Spiritual Beings* absolutely believe in a higher power, they just don't put the higher power in a "religious box," give it a name, sex, or ethnicity. They are usually well versed in many different religions and belief systems because they are always searching for the meaning of life and how they fit in it. These individuals

121

are always open to talk to people from different faiths, religions, belief systems, and backgrounds, because they are constantly open to growth. Some *Spiritual Beings* even incorporate meditation and yoga in their daily life, which are both spiritual in nature.

Spiritual Beings will not completely write you off if you are religious. They understand that they are the minority in the world. They understand that they see things through a completely different lens than the average person. With that being said, even though they won't completely shut a religious potential mate out, they will have expectations of growth. They will want you to explore, learn, and grow in different ways, spiritually, and ultimately find a truth that works for you, not a truth that was given or forced on you.

Health Nut

The *Health Nut* is deeply passionate about following a healthy diet and maintaining an active lifestyle. They monitor each and everything they eat and are always involved in some type of active workout regimen such as cycling, running, swimming, yoga, weight lifting, or some other aerobic or anaerobic activity. When it comes to diet and exercise, they are quite regimented and disciplined. The words mediocrity and complacency are not a part of their lexicon. They are always seeking new ways to improve their overall health. You may

find these individuals to be vegan, pescatarian, or maybe they just don't eat certain foods they have deemed unhealthy for human consumption. Their diet and overall fitness is more than a suggestion, it's a lifelong *Conviction*.

Trash Compacter

The *Trash Compacter* could care less about what they put in their body. They use food for comfort and entertainment versus sustenance. Unlike the *Health Nut*, the *Trash Compacter* lives to eat as opposed to eating to live. They may complain about being obese and out-of-shape, but they never do anything about it. They continue to choose the unhealthiest food choices, and simultaneously complain about how unhealthy they are and sometimes even find it comical. *Trash Compacters* will never attempt to do anything to combat their unhealthy lifestyle until a doctor tells them, "You will have to take medication." Or even worse, "You are going to die if you don't change your diet and become more active." In some cases, even with the possibility of having to take prescription drugs indefinitely or dying, the *Trash Compacter* continues their unhealthy routine because that's what they are accustomed to.

"If all you want to do is sit on the sofa and eat cookies, you should find someone that is going to sit on the sofa and eat cookies with you."
- Shaun

Slobs

Slobs typically don't care about appearances. Pretty much everything in their life is in disarray. They could care less or are indifferent about their personal appearance. If you visit their house, everything appears disheveled. Dirty clothes are everywhere. There are always dirty dishes in the sink and scattered around their living quarters. Their bed is never made. The trash cans are always overflowing. The toilets and bath tubs are always dirty. Worst of all, the lingering stench of the house is unbelievably horrid. If you are brave enough to ride in their car, it's not much different than their home. Some *Slobs* are just junky; others are junky and nasty. Most *Slobs* don't care about how you feel about their seemingly calamitous state of being.

Neat Freaks

Neat Freaks don't function well in the midst of chaos. They purge constantly because they refuse to be hoarders. Everything in their life has a place and a specific function. Depending on the behavior, some *Neat Freaks* are deemed to have (OCD) Obsessive Compulsive Disorder. Like many behaviors, there are various extremes. On one extreme, a *Neat Freak's* house is always clean, and you probably can't eat in their car. On the other extreme, which definitely may be considered OCD, *Neat Freaks* may only use white towels, take

five showers a day, alphabetize their spices in the food pantry, and iron and fold their underwear a certain way, every time. In any case, if they are forced to deviate from their normal orderly routine, it may cause them various levels of discomfort.

Label Whore

Label Whores are highly materialistic people that are all about the show, labels, titles, and attention. Male and female *Label Whores* may differ on the presentation of their materialistic lifestyle, but keeping up with the masses, current trends, and presenting themselves as individuals that only have the best in every area of their life is the common denominator, whether they can afford it or not. They only wear name-brand clothes. They only drive high-end vehicles, which they trade in every two or three years for a more current version. They refuse to vacation at anything less than 5-star hotels. In many cases, the male *Label Whore* is looking for someone to spoil, and his female counterpart (the Gold Digger) is only open to entertaining men that can add to her lavish lifestyle.

Penny-Pinchers

There is a very thin line between being cheap and frugal. Frugal is being savvy and resourceful with your money. Cheap is when you monetarily cut corners to the detriment of yourself or others to prevent yourself from spending money. *Penny-Pinchers* are frugal people who are the antithesis of *Label*

Whores. Sometimes frugal people are perceived as cheap, when in actuality, they just choose not to spend money on things they deem frivolous. It's usually *Penny-Pinchers* that subscribe to the latter.

Penny-Pinchers believe living an opulent lifestyle is wasteful and unnecessary, especially if you don't possess the resources. They describe the aforementioned lifestyle as "living beyond your means." Certain characteristics of *Penny-Pinchers* are: they drive the same modest car for a long time; they prefer to cook over eating out because it's usually healthier and most often eating out is expensive; they very seldom shop for clothes; they hold on to things for a very long time, and if they choose to make a big purchase, they research it thoroughly. *Label Whores* and *Penny-Pinchers* usually don't play well together.

Image Illusionist

Most people are conscious and aware of how they appear to others. The *Image Illusionist* however, is extremely particular about their personal appearance. Whatever appearance they have crafted or manufactured for themselves has to be consistent every time they are seen by the masses. It doesn't matter what is going on; whether it's just running to the grocery store or attending a sit-down dinner, they are going to make sure their appearance is on point. Their appearance is

predicated on more than just clothes, a car, and/or status. It's a daily scam of sorts. Some would even say a façade and it varies between women and men.

> *"My parents have been married for 35 years and my father has never seen my mother without make-up. She always wakes up an hour before him to 'put on her face.'"*
> *- Essence*

The *Image Illusionist* woman may be more sociably accepted only because she's more of a common occurrence. Thus, she has more options at her disposal. This could be considered a *Double Standard*. The most noticeable option is the concept of cosmetics, which is multifaceted. Make-up is the most common. The average woman may or may not wear make-up daily. For the *Image Illusionist*, it is mandatory. This includes, but it is not limited to, lipstick, foundation, concealer, blush, mascara, eye liner, and eye shadow. Also, she may incorporate fake eye lashes, acrylic or gel nails, and colored contacts. That's just part of the canvas. To cap off this ensemble, she may also incorporate some type of wig or hair weave, which includes hair extensions, and lace fronts.

> *"I wear wigs and weave most of the time because I don't want to damage my natural hair. It's called a protective style. I love*

my natural hair. I just like to change it up every once in a while. I like having options."
- Tammy

As far as her physical fitness, she doesn't waste time working out, she just buys what she needs to give her body the illusion that she is in optimal shape. These items include push-up bras, which makes her breasts appear full and firm, girdles that make her stomach and back seem flat, and compression stockings, such as Spanx, that also have a firming effect on her butt and thighs.

Even though creating illusions with their appearance is most prevalent with females, it's not exclusive to females. Men are also *Image Illusionists*. Typically, you may see men that have to be "suited and booted" at all times. Every time you see them, they will always have on a suit, even at a sporting event. That's pretty standard, right? The *Image Illusionist* man takes it a little further.

These men consider their hair an intricate part of their appearance. As they grow older, their hairline either starts to recede or their hair starts to thin out. Instead of embracing the baldness, they elect to get hair plugs, spray hair to cover the bald spots, male hair weaves, or they opt for a hair piece. Additionally, if this man has a physique that is not the most attractive, instead of banging it out in the gym, he chooses to

wear a girdle to disguise his "beer belly," just like his female counterpart does. In addition, a man that beautifies himself further, such as getting manicures, pedicures, facials, and exfoliations may be considered metrosexual, which is generally acceptable. Men that go further by mimicking women (e. g., arching eyebrows, waxing their body, wearing clear nail polish, and wearing body shapers) may consider themselves gender fluid, are homosexual, or are perceived as such.

"Woman do things to enhance their appearance. Why can't we do the same? That's such a Double Standard."
- Blain

A more permanent solution to creating an *Image Illusionist* or manufactured beauty is cosmetic surgery. Both men and women participate in this phenomenon of permanent body augmentation. They don't want to perform the same process every day to achieve the manufactured look they exhibit. Therefore, they seek a more permanent solution - plastic surgery. This could be something as minor as Botox, lip injections, or liposuction surgery. Then you have those that get more invasive procedures such as nose jobs, and breast, penis, and chin implants. Some may perceive *Image Illusionists* as insecure and believe they are suffering from self-hatred. The *Image Illusionist* simply says. "I just like looking a certain way."

Nerds

Many *Nerds* are highly intelligent individuals, but can be socially awkward. The characters of the show *Big Bang Theory* and Steve Urkel of the show *Family Matters* are examples of the quintessential *Nerd*. All these characters are highly intelligent individuals in various areas of arts, sciences, and/or education. Having graduated with terminal degrees at a very young age, some have even made major life discoveries, and are innovators in their field.

Socially, *Nerds* may be into comic books, playing video games, watching sci-fi movies such as *Star Wars* and the *Star Trek Sagas*, as well as participating in other eccentric activities. *Nerds* usually have very high IQ's, are academically minded, and see the world differently than the average person. They are interested in dating, but they are just uncomfortable with the concept. The *Nerd* is highly ambitious and focused on their personal areas of interest. They are probably more comfortable with going to a science convention where the keynote speaker is Stephen William Hawking, an English theoretical physicist, or visiting a planetarium to meet cosmologists, and the astrophysicist, Neil deGrasse Tyson, as opposed to entertaining a possible mate. However, under the right tutelage, *Nerds* can evolve. They welcome that social piece they are missing, because they yearn to be cool, which will make them more

well-rounded people. If and when they acquire the social piece, they may be perceived more as an intellectual versus a *Nerd*.

Baby Boy

Baby Boy is a movie where actor Tyrese Gibson played a character named Jodi who was raised by a single mother, never met his father, had two children by two different women, still lived at home, and didn't have a job. All the women in his life took care of him. The character Jodi epitomizes a *Baby Boy*, which could also be synonymous with a "mama's boy." This condition is spawned over many years of interactions and experiences between mother and son. It's commonly seen when there is a single mother raising her son alone, with no, or very little male influence. Some women tend to raise their daughters and baby their boys. The former tends to create the *Independent Woman*, because they look at the daughter as a younger version of themselves. Thus, the expectations are typically higher because she doesn't want her daughter to repeat her mistakes. The latter leads to creating the *Baby Boy*.

In certain cases where the mother is fulfilling the roles of two parents because the father is absent, the mother may feel guilty and feel the need to compensate by giving her son everything and not holding him accountable to anything. Ultimately, the mother emasculates her son unknowingly.

Ironically, she raises the same type of man that she refuses to date, a man that thinks a woman should take care of him.

The mother also develops a very bizarre attachment with her son, almost like a boyfriend or husband. Unfortunately, a single mother cannot raise a boy to be a man. However, she can raise him to be a good person. So, either the son becomes an unproductive man and never leaves home, or the mother raises a successful adult that leaves home and becomes self-sufficient, but only to a certain extent because the umbilical cord is still attached. Thus, it's very challenging for another woman to be number one in his life. Now, does every single man that was raised solely by his mother qualify as a *Baby Boy*? Absolutely not. However, I have found the *Baby Boy* to be the norm in these situations, not the exception.

Irrationalist

Any behavior that is associated with illogical thought or opinions is considered *Irrational*. *Irrationalists* generally have a hodgepodge of issues and have a least one thing in common: They are out of touch with reality. For this particular *Species*, *Irrationalists* will be qualified under three identifiers: You have those that love to argue, others that seek attention and thrive off drama, and pathological liars.

First there is the arguer who loves to debate all the time. They thrive off of confrontation. It doesn't matter the subject

matter. It could be politics, sports, or religion, they will always be defensive and combative. No matter if they are clearly wrong, they will continue to argue. Additionally, they will make a point to raise their voice thinking that this will help them win the battle. It doesn't matter to them if they look like an idiot or not. Their only objective is to make their point and have their voice heard.

There is always something going on with an *Irrationalist* that loves attention and drama, the second identifier. Every time you turn around, they are either initiating or instigating a messy situation or simply finding themselves in the middle of a messy or petty situation. These situations consist of, but are not limited to, destroying personal property out of jealousy, gossiping about everybody and everything, coming over your house unannounced, always making a scene, or repeatedly calling and leaving you threatening messages until you answer the phone. Often times it's a situation they could have avoided, but they choose to inject themselves or make something out of nothing. Then they have the nerve to play the victim when someone confronts them or calls them out on their shenanigans.

Finally, you have the *Irrationalist* that lies all the time about everything for no apparent reason. Some people believe that a lie is a lie, period. Others believe there are variations or levels of lying. For those individuals that lie, they believe in the latter and they run the gambit. Now, let's delineate various types of lies. There are outright volunteered lies, where an individual makes up stories and scenarios for no apparent reason. Lies of omission, where an individual doesn't necessarily lie, but they omit the truth. Lastly, people tell lies to protect themselves. Omitting the truth and lying to protect yourself seems to be more acceptable. *Irrationalists* that lie most often usually lie all the time, for any reason. They lie so much and so often that they start to believe their own lies. You can never predict what might come out of their mouth. Even if you catch them in a lie, they have a lie or lies to cover up the lie that was exposed.

Over Achievers

Over Achievers are insatiable beings that choose extraordinary over ordinary. They are never completely fulfilled in any area of their life and are usually highly ambitious. Each time they reach a certain milestone in their life, they have already put their next project in motion. This could be a good thing or bad thing.

In a positive light, where education is concerned, they will not only reach the highest levels, they will also be lifelong students because they will incorporate self-study in their daily life. As far as health and wellness, they will constantly strive for the highest level of diet and fitness. As far as adventure,

they are constantly traveling to different countries, experiencing various cultures. They also may be perceived as daredevils because they may participate in "out-of-the-box" activities such as skydiving, scuba diving, rafting, zip-lining, and related adventures. You're probably thinking these types of people are crazy. They are not crazy; they are just bored and always looking for their next high. Ultimately, encounters with *Over Achievers* cause ordinary people to "look at the man in the mirror" and take an inventory of their life's failures and successes. These encounters may be inspirational or depressing.

On the negative side, *Over Achievers* may not do so well in a committed, monogamous relationship. People seeking stable relationships may perceive *Over Achievers* as unstable and uncompromising. Additionally, just like all areas of an *Over Achiever's* life, they get bored very easily. If a person is not able to grab and keep an *Over Achiever's* attention, they may become insecure and dissatisfied with the current situation. It's no one's fault, *Over Achievers* are just always looking to see what's next.

"I'm scared to date you, because you get bored too easy. You might get bored with me."
- Cat

These are just some of the categories of people I've identified from my life experiences and observations. There are a myriad of *Species* in the world. You may or may not identify with any of the *Species* I have outlined and that's okay. The point is that you understand that there are different types of people in the world and it may behoove you to be able to recognize and understand who you share time and space with. Additionally, it may be important to know who and what you are to better understand who and what you're compatible with. You may meet a person that is a divergent, a combination of different *Species*, not necessarily falling into one particular faction. However, at the core, their foundation consists of certain characteristics that are recurring. The other parts are merely layers that may not be as significant. Additionally, people's state of being may be static or fluid.

It's important to pay attention to how you and individuals you deal with may or may not evolve over time. These changes may be negative or positive. It's all relative. It's not only about having the initial assessment and conversation and getting to know each other, but also paying attention, observing, and having a continuous conversation as potential changes manifest themselves. Hopefully you have identified what and who you are, which will hopefully assist you with making the most optimal choice when choosing the right mate.

SOUR GRAPES

BUYER'S REMORSE

U h oh, you just realized you made a gargantuan mistake. You married the wrong person for all the wrong reasons. Well, congratulations! You finally got everything you wished for, all the pomp and circumstance: The *Fairytale* wedding, the cake, the ice sculpture, $2,000 worth of wedding pictures, and angels hanging from the ceiling of the church as you were walking down the aisle in your $8,000 Vera Wang dress. Not just angel figurines, you had people actually dressed as angels hanging from the ceiling. Most importantly, you finally got your *Ring*. Yaaaay!!!!

Okay, okay… maybe you didn't have all those "bells and whistles." Maybe you had something a bit more toned down, or maybe you just went to the court house. Regardless, you finally found your perfect someone, your best friend, your soul mate, or did you? Surprise, surprise... the honeymoon is over, the new

car smell has dissipated, and the person you chose to spend the rest of your life with vanished and someone else appeared. Guess what? They are possibly experiencing similar sentiments. All of sudden you realize they are not the person you thought they were and the *Marriage* is not what you envisioned.

As a result of making a decision to marry someone that was not fully vetted, rushing into an ill-advised *Marriage*, or simply marrying the wrong person, the *Fairytale* life you were dreaming of has turned into an endless nightmare. You are experiencing what I like to refer to as *Buyer's Remorse*. Sometimes coming to the realization that you married the wrong person for whatever reason can be like realizing you made a really bad purchase. However, the refund and exchange policy/process is a little different.

How many times have you seen a pair of shoes, a blouse, or a dress that you just had to have right at that moment? You just couldn't wait, so you purchased the item with very little thought, all emotion no logic. However, when you got home and tried it on under your lights and in front of your mirror, you didn't feel the same level of euphoria you felt at the department store. Not a problem, right? You have the receipt, you can just simply take it back, problem solved.

Or maybe you're looking for your dream house. In this situation, you don't rush into a decision, you do your homework and talk to multiple people with a background in real-estate before making your decision. At least, you thought you did your homework. Shortly after you move in, you realize there are numerous renters in the community that don't take care of their property, which negatively impacts everyone's property value. That was the one thing you forgot to investigate, and it turned out to be a real deal breaker. No problem. You can sell the house and move to another part of town. The difference with a failed *Marriage* versus a disappointing purchase is that dissolving a *Marriage* is not as easy as taking clothes back to a department store for a refund or moving to a new community.

In my opinion, life is not predestined. Life is about choices. Every choice you make leads to another set of choices. Figuratively speaking, each fork in the road you encounter constitutes a potential choice that must be made. You can either stand still or make a move. The choice you make determines your next outcome or station in life. There are a multitude of possible outcomes contingent on the moves you make. If you elect not to make a choice at all, irrevocable time may be lost.

Depending on your station in life and present circumstances, you may be asking yourself a series of questions as it pertains to a failed *Marriage* and *Buyer's Remorse* such as, but not limited to: "Why would anyone just rush into a *Marriage?*" "I don't want to be married anymore, how do I get out?" "Why was I in such a rush to get married?" "Why in the hell did I have a baby with this fool?" "I thought I made the right decision. Where did I go wrong?" "How did I miss that one thing?" and "I'm a divorcee and single mother, what's next?"

> *"Stop complaining about the father of your children. You chose him."*
> *- Omar*

Let's explore a few classic reasons why a woman would enter into a *Marriage* to only experience *Buyer's Remorse* down the line. I know, I know... you're probably asking, "Aren't men a part of these same failed *Marriages?* Don't men experience *Buyer's Remorse?*" The answer is yes and yes. However, the impact of *Buyer's Remorse* is somewhat different for men, which will be discussed further.

> *"I know marrying this person is a mistake, but everything is paid for. All the invitations have been mailed. We have friends and family flying in from everywhere. I guess I will just 'go with the flow' and hope for the best."*
> *- Margaret*

Family Pressure

Every time you visit your parents, you're confronted with a barrage of questions related to when you are getting married and when you're going to have kids. At every family gathering or reunion, it's the same line of questioning. Oh yes, and let's not forget all the other females in your family around your age and younger that are married and on the brink of having child number two. To top it off, all your friends and family members are constantly trying to set you up with eligible bachelors, making you seem lonely and desperate. The recurring questions you ask yourself are: "I can't be the only one without a husband and children, right?" "What am I doing wrong?" and "Is this really my life?" Unfortunately, you become extremely desperate and marry the next man that is fairly decent.

> *"Baby you're almost 40. Your egg carton is empty and if you have any left, they're probably cracked."*
> *- Helen Patterson, Being Mary Jane*

Biological Clock

In your opinion, you did everything right. You went to college and graduated with honors. You have achieved every single career goal you set for yourself. You purchased your first house at 26 and you just acquired that luxury car you've always wanted. Congratulations, you are a successful *Independent Woman*. However, you are alone and you just realized you are not in your 20s anymore and the eggs in your ovaries have an expiration date. You would prefer to be married before having children, but have entertained the idea of acquiring a sperm donor as a last resort. Getting married is your top priority, "by any means necessary."

Surprise Procreation

You're not thinking about getting married or having kids. You are a selfish human being and you are okay with it. You like to have fun, travel, and just do you. You are okay with casual relationships and you are not trying to be tied down. As long as you use contraceptives and practice safe sex, it's all good. Uh oh, the condom broke and now you are in a quandary. You find yourself pregnant with a casual partner. What are your options? Do you keep the baby or have an abortion? You're not a teenager anymore and you have the money and resources to raise a child, so you have no solid justification to get an abortion. However, you really don't want a kid, not right now anyway. But you don't believe in abortion. At the same time, you don't want to have a baby with this dude, he was just a friend with benefits, somebody for right now, not forever.

After countless sleepless nights and conversations with girlfriends and relatives, along with being from a deeply religious family, you decide to marry the individual you accidently procreated with. Your decision is further solidified by the fact that you don't want to be a "baby mamma" and you think the child will have a better life as a result of being raised in a two-parent household. Consequently, you marry your "cuddy buddy," your "friend with benefits."

27 Dresses

You open your closet one day looking for an outfit to wear to the club or maybe you're looking for your workout clothes for an early morning run, and you realize you have participated in 27 weddings, wearing 27 different dresses as a bridesmaid or maid of honor. Everyone around you is married and having babies that you think smell so good and are so cute. All your girlfriends are having baby showers, birthday parties for their infant children, and celebrating various *Marriage* anniversaries. You're secretly jealous of the fact that your best friend and little sister got married before you. You are successful in your professional life, but you feel you have failed constantly in your personal life. You say to yourself "I refuse to participate in any future weddings or wear any maid of honor or bridesmaid dresses." Furthermore, you say, "The next dress I wear is my wedding dress for my own wedding." Subsequently, you rush into matrimony with the very next guy you date.

 **PLAYING FOR THE RING**

"What's wrong with me? I have a degree, my own house, and no children. Why can't I get married? This is some bullshit!!!"
- Toni

Religion

As a highly religious person, your religion guides every aspect of your life. Amongst a multitude of tenets, you've been taught your entire life that sex before *Marriage* is a sin and if you participate in premarital sex, there will be grave consequences such as unwanted pregnancies and STDs. Nonetheless, you authorize oral and/or anal sex in your relationships. However, that's not sufficient. Eventually, your natural urge to copulate takes over and your flesh may have momentary lapses of weakness. Therefore, you either marry your high school sweetheart right after you graduate from high school, or the person that eventually takes your virginity, so that you can have sex without feeling guilty or feeling like you're committing a sin. Or, you may have had sex previously, but at a certain point you decided to practice abstinence and became a "born again virgin" until your wedding night.

"My husband and I followed our faith as it pertained to our relationship. Prior to Marriage, we had a true courtship. We decided not to be intimate until our wedding night. Before we were married, my husband was celibate for 12 years. I practiced abstinence for four years. We dated for three

144

years and never spent any intimate time together, purposefully. We spent quality time together, but before the sun would set, we parted ways so we wouldn't be tempted to have sex. My husband was more adamant about abstaining than I was. We didn't even see each other naked until after we were married. I thought I did everything the right way. Obviously, I did not. My husband does not know how to communicate and I'm bored. Lately, I've been conversing with my high school sweetheart. I'm entertaining the idea of giving him some (sex). I haven't had sex with my husband in a year. I'm also looking for a new place to live. In retrospect, I guess I didn't fully evaluate my decision. Maybe we should have lived together. We definitely should have learned more about each other."

-Abigail

Bamboozled

The day you got married was the happiest day of your life. You thought you were married to the perfect man. He was intelligent, handsome, charismatic, and charming. Additionally, no other man had ever made you have multiple orgasms. You were under the impression that he was a college educated man that was well respected in the community. Shortly after you moved into your dream house you discovered

you were sold a "bill of goods." You married your spouse's "representative."

Not only does your husband have a sketchy past that involves ex-wives and children he conveniently failed to mention, you also discovered he served time in prison for credit card fraud, and on top of all that, he is in the country illegally. Additionally, all the romantic things he did to woo you came to a screeching halt. Okay, okay…that may be an extreme example. Notwithstanding, deception on any level can be devastating. Unfortunately, you were deceived because you didn't fully scrutinize the individual's character and background before entering matrimony. To add insult to injury, you just discovered you were pregnant.

> *"Oh, I say and I say it again, ya been had! Ya been took! Ya been hoodwinked! Bamboozled! Led astray! Run amok!"*
> *- El-Hajj Malik El-Shabazz (Malcolm X)*

Societal Pressures

As a result of societal pressures, you think getting married and having children is what you're supposed to do. Your whole life you've been fed this idea that you should go to college and get married, have 2.5 kids, and buy a house with a white picket fence with a dog. Everyone around you is married and having children, therefore you decided to get married because everybody else is doing it. Thus, the very first chance you have, you get hitched.

"My ex-husband was a wonderful boyfriend, but a horrible husband."

- Laurie

All relationships between men and women are not necessarily meant to be romantic in nature or for that matter result in *Marriage*. Just like milk and/or other perishable items, some people in your life have an expiration date. I firmly believe in the old adage that people are in your life for a reason, season, or a lifetime. You have to be very careful not to confuse those realities. Sometimes you may need to just enjoy the moment, devoid of expectations. If you marry a person that was only supposed to be in your life for a reason or season, there may be problems down the line. The aforementioned scenarios of reasons women get married didn't necessarily have anything to do with true love. They were more about situations of desperation, fear, or miscalculation, which led to *Buyer's Remorse*. When you enter a union out of desperation, fear, or miscalculation, your vision is not 20/20. As a result, you may miss the *Red Flags*, which do not allow you to make an informed choice using logic over emotion.

 **PLAYING FOR THE RING**

"Where did I go wrong? Will I have to pay for this mistake for the rest of my life?"
- Carlotta

SPOILED MILK

RED FLAGS

Red Flags are those signs you see in the early stages of a courtship that may indicate present and/or future problems with a person. You may overlook the *Red Flags* because experiencing the potential *Fairytale* wedding overshadows the alarming *Red Flags* that present themselves. These *Red Flags* are overlooked because in most situations decisions are being made utilizing emotion versus logic which contributes to *Buyer's Remorse*. Let's look at some *Red Flags* to watch out for in broad categories, with specific examples. I've also provided potential repercussions of ignoring said *Red Flags*.

Infidelity

🚩 When you were dating him, you were the *Side Piece* and he was married.

🏴 When you met him, he was a public figure (athlete, politician, entertainer...) with countless female admirers.

Repercussions: He cheats on you. He has nude pictures of women on his cell phone. He has a child outside of the *Marriage*. He has another family that he takes care of. He was never a one-woman man. If he cheated on a woman to be with you, the likelihood that he will cheat on you with someone else is almost certain.

Abusive

🏴 He was arrested for domestic violence in a previous relationship, however he explained to you that he was a changed man and it would never happen again.

🏴 The first time you had a disagreement with him, he became enraged, used profane language, grabbed you aggressively, and pushed you onto the bed.

🏴 Whenever he gets upset, he breaks things.

Repercussions: You find yourself in the emergency room with multiple injuries. He also abuses your children.

Poor Communicator

🏴 He could have a conversation about every subject under the sun, except his feelings for you.

🏴 He changed the subject whenever uncomfortable conversations came up.

🏴 He got upset and walked away whenever topics came up that he didn't agree with.

Repercussions: Whenever you have an issue, you either argue or don't discuss it all. Ultimately the problems continuously get worse.

Control Freak

🏴 He expressed that he preferred to date younger women because they were teachable.

🏴 He called to check on you every 30 minutes, and you thought it was romantic.

🏴 He never wanted you to spend time with your family and friends.

🏴 When you went out to eat, he always ordered for you.

🏴 He always had an opinion about your appearance, how you should wear your hair, and how you should dress.

Repercussions: As you age, you crave more independence. He remains the same. He wants to know where you are at all times. Ultimately, he puts a tracking device on your car and spyware on your cell phone. He doesn't want you to evolve.

Liar

🏴 He lied about being associated with various organizations.

🏴 He claimed to know luminaries and politicians he never met.

🏴 He lied about not having children.

🏴 He lied on his taxes.

🏴 You've witnessed him lie to close family and friends.

🏴 He lied about being in a certain profession.

🏴 He lied about his level of education to impress you.

Repercussions: He lies about where he goes, who he's with, and what he does. You were under the impression that he would never lie to you.

Financially Irresponsible

🏴 He didn't pay his bills on time.

🏴 He had a 400-credit score.

🏴 He constantly overdrew his checking account.

🏴 He owned a luxury car, but lived with his parents.

🏴 He had problems making car payments, thus he was constantly hiding his car so it would not be repossessed.

🏴 He had children from a previous relationship that he refused to take care of financially.

Repercussions: He defaults on household utilities habitually. He makes big ticket purchases without consulting with you. He has a problem saving money. His check is being garnished for back child support payments. As a result of his irresponsible financial decisions, he has bad credit, thus everything is in your name (e.g., car and house).

RED FLAGS

Unhealthy

- You never witness him eat a fruit or vegetable.
- He expressed that he hated the taste of water.
- His idea of exercising was having sex.
- He ate meat and potatoes every day.
- He drank some form of alcohol on a daily basis to wind down after work.

Repercussions: He becomes obese. He develops preventable diseases such as high blood pressure, diabetes, and high cholesterol. He ultimately has a poor quality of life as far as his health is concerned or simply experiences an untimely death. Thus, you are alone.

Limited Ambition

- Education was never a priority and he felt that school was not for everybody, including him.
- He never finished anything he started (e.g., degrees, certifications, licenses, household projects, and entrepreneurial endeavors).
- He never had a career you wanted him to have.
- When you met him, he was selling weed.
- He was always expecting the "hook up" (e.g., free stuff, discounted items, and stolen products).
- He was a grown man still aspiring to be a rapper or producer, living in his grandmother's basement.

🚩 He was always soliciting friends and families to participate in the current pyramid scheme or multi-marketing scheme (e.g., Amway, Bodi by Vi, Noni Juice, and Legal Shield).

"If I die who will take care of my children. Clearly my ex-husband is ill-equipped for parenthood. He can barely take care of himself."
- India

Repercussions: As a result of not being able to establish a steady income, he is unable to contribute financially on a constant basis. He doesn't feel like a real man because he can't provide for his family. He starts to suffer from depression, which causes him to self-medicate with drugs and alcohol and/or abandons his family.

Down Low

🚩 Every time you had sex, he preferred anal sex over vaginal sex.

🚩 You caught him trying on your lingerie.

🚩 He was always with his best friend or homeboys, spending more time with them than you.

🚩 He's always went on trips with the fellas, but seldom travels with you.

🚩 He loves going shoe shopping with you.

- He has always over accessorized. For example, every outfit he wears consists of matching hat, sunglasses, belt, and shoes.
- He's never had a unibrow, but still arched/waxed his eyebrows.
- Whenever you went out, it took him longer to get dressed than you.

Repercussions: You discover that he likes to sleep with women as well as men. He was using you to disguise the fact that he was homosexual, bisexual, or a *Double Agent.*

Baby Boy

- He never had a father or positive male figure in his life.
- His mother, grandmother, aunts, and sisters always catered to him.
- As an adult, his mother would always come to his house to clean, cook, and do laundry.

Repercussions: He expects you to wait on him as if you are his personal maid, just like his mother. He also has to consult with his mother before he makes any major life decision.

It boils down to this, when a person tells you or shows you who they are, believe them the first time. Do not create your own reality. If you think you are going to change them, you are wasting your time. A person only changes if they choose to change. Teach a person how you want to be treated and vice versa. Now you have tied the knot and you are miserable, reflecting on the *Red Flags* that you saw, but dismissed. What's your next move?

> *"If I get a divorce, I will be perceived as a failure."*
> *- Belinda*

As a result of ignoring *Red Flags* you are unhappy with your *Marriage*. Your challenge is to make the most ideal decision for your situation. You can either stay or go. So, you may think the most obvious decision is to cut your losses and file for divorce. Depending on your situation, that may be easier said than done. Yes, if you haven't been married long and you have not procreated, an uncontested divorce may be appropriate. However, if there are other variables, you may elect to stay in a loveless *Marriage*.

> *"I don't want to hurt the kids. It's not their fault. I guess I will wait until they graduate from high school and leave home, then I will divorce him."*
> *- Courtney*

Roommates

You really want a divorce, but you find that your whole life is intertwined with another person, whom you despise. Not only do you have joint banks accounts, and a mortgage in both names, you also have children. So, you start to play out various

scenarios. Dissolving bank accounts, that's pretty easy. Selling the house and splitting the proceeds to keep your credit intact could be a prolonged process, but plausible.

"If I would have known my Marriage was going to end in divorce, I would have kept my house from when I was single."
- Issa

Now, how do you handle children? You can't just split them in half and give 50% to each spouse. So, you decide to stay for the kids. Essentially, you're roommates in a symbiotic relationship. You don't have sex anymore and you sleep in separate rooms. You justify staying in a lifeless *Marriage* because you feel that it's not the children's fault that their parents have irreconcilable differences, and they should not be penalized by not living in a household with both parents.

"You have to make a choice. The longer you wait to leave, the deeper the proverbial hole becomes. Consequently, it will be more challenging to climb out."
- Sanchez

Cheat

So, the kids' lives are uninterrupted and they remain happy and are oblivious to what is really happening. However, you are still miserable because the interaction between you and your spouse has not improved. To the outside world (friends, family, co-workers...), you have the perfect *Marriage*. As a person that takes her *Marriage* vows seriously, you fight the urge to cheat on your spouse. You could care less about the man himself, but the institution of *Marriage* is still very sacred to you. After weighing the possible consequences of infidelity, you finally decide to fill that void. However, as we discussed earlier, cheating will probably only add fuel to the fire of what your *Marriage* has become.

> *"Marrying my ex-husband was categorically the worst decision I have ever made in my life. The only good thing that came out of it were my children. If I could go back and change who their father is, I would. If I knew then, what I know now, we would have never even had a conversation."*
> *- Marsha*

Divorce

After years of, "should I stay or should I go," you finally decide to purge your life and file for divorce. *Free at last, free at last, thank god almighty, I'm free at last!* However, you never thought you would be a single mother, and more importantly, you still have to deal with your ex because you have children together. Wow, how does that look?

> *"Go ahead, file for divorce. No one is going to want your old fat ass with three kids anyway."*
> *- Simon*

CHAMPAGNE

NEW NORMAL

So, you loved being married and the idea of family life. You enjoyed the idea of coming home to someone you adored, dinner parties, cuddling on the sofa, family vacations, celebrating special occasions and if you have children, you enjoyed the fact that you were raising your children in a two-parent home. After a while, you just didn't love who you were married to anymore. Initially, you chose to stay because you did not want to be perceived as a failure. You always said, "I will never be a baby mama." Yet you find yourself in a situation that may be perceived as such.

When you first entered your *Marriage*, you just knew it would be for a lifetime. You never thought you would have to deal with the dating game anymore. The thought of having to use condoms again is very aggravating, but necessary. On top of that, you have a kid or kids that are, or should be your top priority. If you could snap your fingers and fill the vacancy left by your ex-husband with a man that you're more compatible with and loves your kids, you would, but it's not necessarily that easy or realistic.

> *"If you plan on dating me, you have to date my kids as well. We come as a package deal."*
> *- Kinshasa*

How will you juggle family life as a single mother, interaction with your ex-husband, and possible male interests? When should you let men meet your children? How long should you wait to date? Should you date at all while your children are young and still living in the home? Should you go back to your maiden name? This is definitely a *New Normal* you never thought you would have to experience.

> *"I'm not sure if I should keep my husband's last name or go back to my maiden name. I don't know how I feel about having a different last name than my children. At the same time, I don't want to keep his last name either."*
> *- Camille*

Fairytale Deferred

Well, the *Fairytale* life you imagined did not work out how you envisioned. You're now realizing that the dress, cake, extravagant wedding, and *Ring* were not that big of a deal, especially after experiencing a failed *Marriage*. Now that you are out of a state of denial and have accepted your new reality, hopefully the transition to your *New Normal* will be a bit easier. Don't fret, it's okay, life must and will go on, it just may take a while to adjust. However, you may have to recalibrate what you're seeking as it relates to a potential mate and everyday family life.

Modified *Wish List*

Remember that list of things you were looking for in a man when you were younger, before *Marriage* and children? Have they changed? Are the variables in your life different? Once you have answered these questions, let's look at your possible options.

Option 1: You could relinquish total custody of your children to your ex-spouse and start a new life with a new husband and new family, or stay single.

Option 2: You could be a serial dater that dates different men with no strings attached, with no intentions of your children ever meeting them.

Option 3: You could compartmentalize your life and keep your children and the man or men you date completely separate in two different worlds until your children are grown and gone.

Option 4: You could choose not to date at all until your children are grown and gone.

Option 5: You could elect to date and not tell the man you are dating about your children until the relationship matures to a certain level.

Option 6: You could seek to date seriously with intentions to marry and form a blended family.

In many situations where there is a divorce and children are involved, the reality for each spouse is quite different. The children usually live with the mother primarily. The father is tagged with alimony and child support and usually only spends time with the child/children on the weekends, summertime when school is out, and holidays. The father has somewhat of a fresh start and is free to date and basically live the single life. With boundless time, he is free to entertain an array of females for the possibility of matrimony or simply recreation. When women meet him, there are no baby seats in the car and his home is basically set up as a bachelor's pad.

"We just got a divorce, how did he move on to another relationship so fast?"
- Candice

In contrast, the mother essentially becomes a single mother that takes on the daily responsibilities of both parents. This includes but is not limited to cooking, cleaning, yard work, car maintenance, assisting with homework, chauffeuring kids to and from school, and extracurricular activities. Basically, all the things that go along with running a household and raising children, which at one time was the duty of two parents, is now the responsibility of one. Simultaneously, the mother is trying to figure out if and how she will maintain a relationship that is romantic in nature. Her free time is limited, thus dating and getting to know a new man with the hopes of any type of relationship is limited, including *Marriage*.

When making decisions, there are different ways to measure what choice will be best for your situation. We will evaluate the cost-benefit of the aforementioned options by looking at the possible pros and cons of each decision. Pros and cons may vary for each individual's situation. These are merely examples. Let's see how each option may possibly play out.

Fresh Start

Even though most women typically get custody of their children, electing to allow the man to have custody is a possibility. You may not want the responsibility of raising a child alone because you didn't sign up to be a single mother. This option would allow you to have somewhat of a fresh start, without having the daily responsibilities of raising children. This is probably the least likely to happen, but it is possible. How does making a fresh start measure up?

163

"I love motherhood, but I am a career oriented woman with a very important position at a Fortune 500 company. I told my husband if we ever get divorced, the kids are going with him, because I refuse to be a single mother."
- Martina

Option 1: Fresh Start
Pros
You are not weighed down with the daily responsibility of having to take care of someone by yourself.
You have the freedom to go and come as you please.
If you choose to go back to your maiden name, you don't have to explain or be embarrassed about having a different name than your children.
You won't be perceived as a "baby mama."
If *Marriage* is still on your agenda, you may have a better chance of finding a mate.
Cons
Your ex essentially has more influence over how your children will be raised.
You may miss certain stages of your children's maturation.
People may perceive you to be a bad mother because you allowed your ex to have full custody of the children.
You may miss your children abundantly and feel very lonely at times.
You may have to pay child support.

No Strings

So, you supposedly got your *Fairytale*, right? You had the wedding, got your *Ring*, experienced the married life and procreated. Right now, you are over it. The only thing you don't regret about your *Marriage* experience is the child/children you produced with your ex-spouse. You are not interested in anything serious, you just want to have fun. Your full disclosure to every guy you meet, date, or hangout with is that you are not looking for anything serious, you have no expectations, and you let them know that they can never come to your house. You feel uncomfortable allowing men to meet your children and you may or may not divulge that you even have children. Also, you may date one or more men at any given time, yes, a rotation. How does that look?

Option 2: No Strings
Pros
The possibility of you becoming attached to one particular person is limited.
You're not in a committed relationship, so you have more time to not only concentrate on your kids, but you can also focus on yourself.
Cons
You may be perceived as a promiscuous woman.
You may get emotionally attached to one of the men, but the feelings are not reciprocated, because that was not an option in the original agreement.

Compartmentalizing

You're a single mother and you are okay with the idea of being a single mother. You are in no rush to be in a committed relationship. However, unlike the no strings option, you only want to entertain one man at a time, because you don't want to be perceived as promiscuous. If a relationship materializes, cool, if it doesn't, that's cool as well. You love being a mother, but at the same time, mama has to let her hair down and have some grown up fun. However, you are not necessarily ready to allow a new man into your child's/children's life, unless you are convinced that it is long-term. The main situation you want to avoid is having multiple men come in and out of your children's life, which may have a negative effect on their overall development. How will compartmentalizing your life work for you?

Option 3: Compartmentalizing
Pros
You don't have to worry about scaring men off by telling them you have children.
You can raise your children without interrupting their normalcy by introducing a non-biological man into their life.
Cons
You're living in two separate worlds, basically living a double life, which may become exhausting.
By keeping these two worlds separate, if you ever want to bring the worlds together, the man may or may not be in compliance, because he likes the situation as is, an arrangement which he believes is no strings attached.

Solo

You're not just over relationships, you're over sex and men all together. You feel that a man and unprotected sex put you in the predicament you are in now. Your one and only priority is raising your children and making sure they become productive citizens in society. Besides you don't have time to entertain a man anyway because you would feel guilty. All your time should be devoted to doing something constructive with your children, right? As far as a women's sexual needs that need to be met, you prefer to visit the local sex store to purchase a dildo, vibrator, or both. How would that work?

Option 4: Solo
Pros
You can concentrate and dedicate the majority of your time and energy to your children.
You don't have to worry about getting emotionally attached to another man.
Cons
You may feel lonely from lack of male companionship.
You may become so focused on your children that you lose yourself. Thus, as they get older and more independent, you don't know what to do with your extra time.
Sex toys cannot completely replace a warm-blooded man.

Bamboozled

You absolutely hate the single life and raising children by yourself. Your preference is to be married again, but you know it may be a challenge having a blended family. You don't want to rush into anything, but you do want companionship. However, you choose not to divulge the fact that you have children because you don't want to scare men away. As a result, you elect not to tell men that you encounter that you have children unless the relationship evolves into something more long term. Does this make sense? Is this fair?

Option 5: Bamboozled
Pros
You can date without the pressure of telling men about your children unless it becomes serious.
You don't have to worry about introducing your children to a potential mate and being apprehensive about if they are going to get along.
Cons
The man may feel deceived because you didn't tell him about the kids initially. As a result, you scare him away.
It may be very challenging to live in two different worlds and not allow one world to find out about the other.

Blended Family

Even though you absolutely hated everything about your *Marriage*, except the birth of your children, you still want to be married. You loved the married life, just not the person you were married to. Casual relationships, just dating to be dating, friends with benefits, or whatever tag or phrase you want to use for arbitrary relationships is not an option. You may not want

to get married immediately, but *Marriage* is the goal and it is non-negotiable.

Option 6: Blended Family
Pros
You gain a household with two parents versus one.
You don't have to handle the day-to-day duties by yourself.
You are in a monogamous relationship and you don't have to deal with casual dating, which you despise.
You have a male presence in your home, which makes you feel safe.
You will not be perceived as a "baby mama."
Cons
The man may not get along with the kids.
The kids may not get along with the man.
The kids may like the new guy more than their biological father because the new guy has more of a positive influence.
The new guy may not get along with the biological father.
It's a possibility that your new boyfriend or husband may molest your child, boy or girl.

"If your child accuses your boyfriend/husband of molestation or rape, who will you believe? The child could be lying or telling the truth. Are you going to choose the child or the man?"

- Amina

Children

With your understanding of how challenging it is to raise children as a single mother, how do you feel about dating someone who also has kids? While you're weighing your options of if and how you will date, you may also want to evaluate whether or not you want to date a man with or without children. Let's look at how dating or eventually marrying a man with children may look.

Men With Children
Pros
He will most likely understand your daily lifestyle, because he also has children.
If he has children and is actively involved in their lives, it's a good chance that he values family.
If he is an active father, he is probably caring and unselfish.
Cons
His time may be just as limited as yours, because he also has children (dating phase).
Your children may not get along, which will make a blended family very challenging.
Depending on the age, sex, sexual orientation, and overall mindset of the children, merging their lives may yield negative results (e.g., fights, resentment, and molestation).
If the relationship doesn't work out, it will be a multiple parting of ways, not just two people.

"I don't want to date anyone with kids. I know it's hypocritical, but I have my own children and I don't want to have to deal with other people's crumb snatchers."

- Egypt

The general assumption may be that people who have children prefer to only date people with children. That is not always the case. If you date a man without kids, how might that play out?

Men Without Children
Pros
He has an abundance of time because he is only responsible for himself.
You don't have to deal with drama from a mother they are no longer in a relationship with.
Cons
He doesn't have children, so he probably won't understand your day-to-day lifestyle.
In general, single men without children may be selfish and self-centered.
He may be commitment phobic because he enjoys his single life.
Since he has an abundance of time and no children, he has time to possibly entertain additional females (rotation).
He may want children and you can't or choose not to have anymore.

"I know I should desire to be in a relationship with a man that's educated and industrious, with no children. However, I prefer to be with the opposite. The single educated man with no children would always have the edge over me. I always want to have the upper hand. Please don't judge me."
- Alexus

Once you have weighed all your options, looking at all the possible advantages and disadvantages of each potential choice, now you can make an informed decision. Your first choice may or may not yield the results you had anticipated and you may have to reevaluate what your next move will be and possibly choose a different option. Another choice may be more appropriate for your situation. Ultimately it will be a constant balancing act between parenthood and your love life.

When you find yourself in a situation where you are thinking about whether you should date, how you should date, should you marry again, and/or how your choices will affect the rearing of your children, you may want to apply the methodologies I have provided. If it does not work for you, no problem, but find a method that does, so that you can make an informed decision. Also, don't be afraid to share your cautionary tale with women that may be going through a similar situation, or adolescent girls to help prevent them from making similar mistakes. Not only can you make improvements in personal areas that are deficient, you can also help others with lessons learned from the relationship/*Marriage* process. Additionally, identifying personal pillars and recognizing similar standards in others may be beneficial to you as well.

172

WATER

CONVICTIONS

Originally, I titled this chapter *1000 Questions*. I felt that it was vital that individuals not wait until after matrimony, cohabitation, and/or procreation to ask pertinent questions that should have been addressed prior to a life altering decision. At that point, it is really too late.

When I was in the process of constructing 1000 questions, a feeling of monotony came over me. Then I thought to myself, "If I'm bored typing these questions, I'm sure a person reading these questions will be bored as well." At that moment, it came to me. When you first meet a person and you're getting to know them, why do you ask each other questions? You ask questions for the purpose of getting to know each other and to gain an understanding or knowledge of what they use to guide their lives, and their various philosophies - what makes them tick? I refer to this guide or moral compass as an individual's overall set of *Convictions*.

Now, before we continue, I need you to ask yourself a very essential and introspective question: "What are your *Convictions*?" Have you ever pondered the concept? Maybe you have, maybe you haven't. Do you even comprehend what a *Conviction* is? If you haven't and you don't understand, not a problem, you will shortly.

By definition, a *Conviction* is a firmly held belief or opinion. What beliefs do you possess that you will never waver on, no matter the circumstances? Your beliefs, the lenses with how you view life have been shaped by your family, level of education, and life experiences. Some parts of your beliefs may even be intuitive.

For example, an individual that identifies themselves as heterosexual cannot fathom the thought of being in any type of same sex arrangement. A person that is vegan is repulsed at the site of animal flesh. One more - a woman that feels she needs to wear make-up to look beautiful or to enhance her looks, would not be caught dead with her face not fully made up. Those are *Convictions*, and typically a person's *Convictions* never change. You must understand what you truly believe individually before you can honestly know what you want in another person.

CONVICTIONS

Whether you have delineated what your *Convictions* are or not, you have them. Everybody lives by a set of individual laws that help them function in various areas of life. Again, variables that contribute to your *Convictions* are usually family influences, education, and life experiences. If you are not able to articulate exactly what your *Convictions* are, having conversations and asking specific questions of yourself and a potential mate may assist you. It's not just about asking an abundance of questions. It's about asking the right questions, which will help you understand who you are associated with. The following categories of questions may assist you in your journey. The questions in each category are geared toward men from women, but are interchangeable.

Marriage

- Are you used to having a rotation of women?
- Can you be with just one person?
- How do you qualify infidelity?
- Have you cheated in a relationship before?
- Do you believe in open relationships?
- Do you believe that people are inherently monogamous?
- How do you feel about polygamy?

"I do not think monogamy is natural. However, I do believe it is a choice. I have been married for 10 years and every morning I make the decision to be monogamous. If I don't make this daily commitment, it's possible for me to fall prey to infidelity."

- Coretta

It's important that you know what a person's concept of *Marriage* consists of so that you can minimize misunderstandings in the future. Some individuals may present themselves in one way as it pertains to *Marriage* to satisfy others' expectations, yet have an alternative secret life.

Standard Operating Procedure

- How do you handle stress?
- How do you handle disappointment?
- How do you handle depression?
- How do you handle rejection?
- How do you handle success?
- What do you usually do when you get angry?
- If you discovered that your significant other cheated on you, what would you do?

"If I came home and caught my wife having sex with someone, I would not kill them because I'm not going to jail, there's no vagina in jail. However, I would beat them both within an inch

of their lives. Next, I would drag them out the house butt naked, tie them up to a tree, urinate on their faces, spread peanut butter and jelly on their bodies covered with slices of white bread, making them human peanut butter and jelly sandwiches. Then I would take all my clothes off, cover myself with baby oil and white flour, put a footie (sock) on one foot and a flip-flop on the other, put on my son's birthday hat with some swimming goggles, and a tool belt around my waist with a beeper. Finally, I would take my daughter's tri-cycle, climb onto the roof of my house and ride around in a circle, sucking on a sour apple Ring-pop, singing YMCA, by the Village People. When I go to court the judge is going to ask the officer what happened. The officer is going to tell the judge what he witnessed when he arrived on the scene. The judge will look at me with a blank stare and say, 'Sir, clearly you are crazy. I'm sentencing you to six months in a mental institution. At the end of six months you will be re-evaluated. Court adjourned.'"

- Norman

- What would you do if you procreated with someone you didn't care about?

- How do you handle death?

A standard operating procedure, or SOP, is an established procedure that is followed in a particular situation. In relationships, you may want to know how a person may potentially react when faced with various circumstances.

Constructive Criticism

- Can you handle constructive criticism?
- Are you checkable?
- Are you a person that identifies and addresses personal deficiencies?

Knowing if a person can accept constructive criticism or not is an indication of whether a person is willing to grow or stay stagnant as a result of having too much pride and not enough humility.

Goals

- What are your short-term and long-term goals?
- What goals have you reached recently?
- What goals would you like to accomplish before *Marriage*?
- What goals would you like to accomplish in a *Marriage*?

Understanding a person's track record of setting and reaching various goals will give you an indication of their personal growth and the potential trajectory of their growth in a relationship.

Freaky Curriculum

- How often do you prefer to have sex?

- Do you enjoy giving and/or receiving oral sex?

- Do you like anal sex?

- Is oral sex mandatory in a relationship?

"So, you don't give head huh? Don't worry, you don't have to give him head, but do understand, he's going to get it from somebody."
- Jimmy

- Do you like to "role play" and multiple sex positions?"

- How do you feel about participating in alternative lifestyles such as threesomes, orgies, and swinging?

- Do you have any fetishes (e.g., urophilia and sadism)?

- How would you keep your sex life exciting in a monogamous relationship?

Knowing a person's sexual preferences is important to make sure you are sexually compatible to prevent potential problems, such as a boring sex life, no sex life, or infidelity.

Homosexuality

- Have you ever sucked a penis?

- Has a man ever performed fellatio on you?

- Do you enjoy anal stimulation?

- Have you ever had any type of sexual relations with a man, transgender, transsexual, or any other type of person other than a natural born woman?

- Have you ever had the urge to have sexual relations or contact with a man?

Completely understanding a person's sexual history and preferences is important because it may not match your personal preferences and values. If you never ask pertinent questions related to homosexuality and it comes to light one day, your partner can always justify their actions by saying, "You never asked."

Sexually Transmitted Diseases (STDs)

- How many sexual partners have you had?
- Have you ever contracted a sexually transmitted disease?
- Do you presently have a sexual transmitted disease?
- Do you practice safe sex?

If not treated properly, some sexually transmitted diseases can be transferred to future partners, years after it was contracted. Additionally, some sexually transmitted diseases can affect future pregnancies and a person's overall health over a lifetime.

Sexual Assault

- Have you ever been raped and/or molested by a family member, friend, or stranger?
- If you were raped and/or molested, where is this person now?

180

- Is the person that raped and/or molested you affiliated with your friends and family?
- Do you ever interact with the person that raped and/or molested you?
- How has your painful experience impacted your life?
- Do you feel you have used your traumatic situation as a crutch or motivation?

It's important to know if a person is psychologically impacted by a sexual assault from their past, because it may negatively affect personal relationships. Also, it's important to know if the person that attacked them is still present and interacting in any immediate circles. They have the propensity to commit the same act with the younger generation.

"I was molested by my uncle when I was younger. I was scared to tell because I didn't think anyone would believe me."
- Maria

Finances

- What type of debt do you possess?
- Do you pay alimony or child support?
- What is your credit score?
- How many personal credit cards do you have?
- Do you pay your bills on time?
- Do you have any investments?

- Do you have life insurance?
- How many streams of income do you have?
- Are you frugal and prefer to save money or are you materialistic and prefer to splurge?
- How do you think bills should be paid in a *Marriage*?

Knowing a person's spending habits and financial history is important, because when you merge your life with another individual, their good and bad financial habits may possibly impact your life.

"I don't believe a man should pay all the bills if the woman is generating a significant income. However, I don't necessarily believe that bills should be paid 50/50 in a Marriage either. I think bills should be paid according to each person's monthly income. For example, if one person makes $6,000/month and their spouse makes $4,000/month, the payment of monthly bills should reflect. So, each person can have their individual accounts and a joint account for the purpose of paying family bills. Therefore, if the monthly expenses (mortgage, utilities, insurance, savings...) are $6,000, the person with the higher salary will be responsible for paying $4,000 and the other spouse will pay $2,000. Once all the bills are paid, each person is free to do whatever they desire with their residual income."
- Muhammad

Health

- What is your medical history?
- What is your family's medical history (mental health, preventable diseases...)?
- What's your HIV status?
- Do you get regular medical check-ups?
- Have you had a major surgery?
- Do you presently have any life threatening or preventable diseases?
- Are you predisposed to any diseases?
- Do you eat to live or live to eat?
- Do you typically cook or eat out?
- What type of foods do you consume?
- Do you prepare healthy meals daily?
- How much water do you drink per day?
- Do you have a sedentary or active lifestyle?
- How often do you work out?
- Do you consume alcohol, smoke, or use any type of illegal or legal drugs?

Everybody is going to die one day. In the game of life, "Father Time" is undefeated. That is a fact. How you're going to die will vary for each person. While you are here, you have a choice about what your quality of life will be, to a certain extent. Understanding a person's overall health will give you an idea of what your quality of life will be as a family unit. Whether you're healthy or unhealthy, it will affect the entire family. If you're both unhealthy, you will probably pass the same unhealthy habits to your offspring and the entire family will potentially experience obesity, high blood pressure, high cholesterol and other preventable diseases. If you are both healthy, you will potentially experience a great quality of life, health wise. If you have completely different views on health and fitness and if neither person chooses to change, that may present a huge problem.

Family

- Were you raised in a one or two parent home?
- Were you raised in an abusive household?
- How is your relationship with your father, mother, and siblings?
- Did your parents believe in corporal punishment?
- Were you raised with pets?
- Did your parents send you to public or private school?
- If your parents needed full-time attention due to declining health, would you prefer to put them in a senior living facility or have them live with you?

Knowing a person's family background and how they were raised may give you some insight into how a person may function in a family and raise their own children.

Procreation & Children

- Do you have any children?
- Have you ever impregnated someone?
- Would you like to have children?
- How many children do you want?
- How do you feel about adoption?
- How do you feel about breastfeeding?
- How do you feel about children getting immunization shots?
- Have you ever aborted a child?
- Would you ever ask your wife to get her tubes tied?
- Would you ever consider getting a vasectomy?

Being aware of a person's situation and views as it relates to procreation and children is important because your plans may not coincide with each other. In some situations, because of circumstances, the willingness to procreate may be there, but it may be biologically impossible.

Organization

- Do you consider yourself organized or unorganized?
- How often do you clean your house?
- Do you have a problem with leaving dirty dishes in the sink?
- Do you make up your bed before you leave home daily?

Some people are complete *Slobs*. Everything in their life is out of order. Other individuals are *Neat Freaks*. They are constantly cleaning everything. Understanding a person's level of organization and cleanliness or lack thereof is important so that you know what you can handle, no matter what your stance is.

Thought Process

- When making decisions, do you utilize more logic or emotion?
- Would you consider yourself a more conscious (deep) thinker or surface thinker?
- Do you function in life as if you're playing checkers, one move at a time, or chess, thinking about multiple moves simultaneously, staying ahead of the game?

Understanding a person's thought process and how they connect the dots in life is paramount to the success of any relationship. It is of the upmost importance when making decisions that will impact the entire family.

Belief Systems

- What is the purpose of life?
- Are you spiritual or religious?
- Do you understand the difference between spirituality and religion?
- Do you subscribe to a particular religion?

- Do you consistently attend classes or services at a religious building?

- Is it important that your spouse share your beliefs?

- Do you plan to raise your children to practice your belief system?

- When you die, would you like to be buried or would you prefer to be cremated?

- What do you think happens when you die?

The area of belief systems or religion can be very divisive. It is imperative that you be on the same page as it relates to what type of religion or belief system will be utilized to govern your household. Many people that practice a religion think that their religion is the right and only religion. To say the least, having discussions about a person's religion can be a very touchy subject. It may even be a major deal breaker. Knowingly and unknowingly, many religious people allow their religion to guide their lives, regardless of whether this makes sense to them or not.

Many *Convictions* are drawn from this way of thinking. However, it may or may not be a *Conviction* because religion is very ritualistic, therefore a person may go through the motions but may not necessarily make a particular tenet or commandment applicable to their lives. "Why," you ask? They are not truly convicted.

 **PLAYING FOR THE RING**

True *Convictions* are static in nature. There is no wavering. Many people have not actively thought about what their *Convictions* truly are. In my life, I have found that most people are constantly looking for someone or something to guide their lives, instead of being *Independent Thinkers*. It allows them to not have personal accountability. The aforementioned series of questions can assist you in determining what your *Convictions* are and if they are compatible with a potential mate.

You're probably asking, "How do I know if they are telling the truth?" You won't know, but you can at least have the conversations and observe the responses. Along with observation and interrogation, you must incorporate discernment and more importantly, time. Also, don't just focus on what they are saying. Pay attention to how they respond and monitor their energy, body language, and other non-verbal cues. Hopefully, after spending time and space with a person, and having a series of conversations, you will find that you are mostly compatible, or not. If so, now you may want to put your relationship to the test before moving forward. It may be a challenging endeavor. Hey, no one said this process would be easy.

PURPLE APPLE

PLEDGE PROCESS

Like many things in life, relationships and *Marriage* are a process, a continuous process. A process, which if not taken seriously can bring about a lifetime of pain and regrets. Some of the most important decisions you have made or will make in life are contingent on a process. There is a basic process associated with applying for a job, searching for a new car, purchasing a new house, or even going shopping for clothes. Your preparation and the vetting process utilized will have a profound effect on how successful or unsuccessful the outcome will be.

More extensive processes are also prevalent with institutions, such as completing basic training before entering the military, satisfying various criteria when pursuing various levels of education, trying out for the school band, and competing in sports camps and athletic competitions for the

opportunity to play for various sports teams on all levels. With many of these institutions, if individuals that are not properly prepared seep through the cracks, they are eventually exposed for who they truly are and are ultimately dismissed.

Another institution that utilizes a process are fraternal organizations. As a member of a fraternal organization that utilizes an expansive process to assess potential members, I have a true understanding of the aforementioned philosophy. As a part of a *Pledge Process*, potential members not only have to satisfy various tasks, they must also complete these tasks as a cohesive unit, known as a line, which encompasses line brothers. The process is not perfect, but if done effectively, not only will these individuals be productive members of the organization, they will also have a bond that may never be broken.

The concept of a process has always been apparent to me, whether it was playing sports, obtaining various degrees, or entering the military. However, the impact of my *Pledge Process* became very clear in the winter of 2014. Three of my line brothers and I traveled to Pontiac, Michigan to attend a double funeral to support another line brother. His father and grandmother died within a few days of each other. We don't see each other often, however, when we get together it's like we saw each other the day before, never skipping a beat.

PLEDGE PROCESS

While in Pontiac, we stayed in a suite at a local hotel. I noticed that every time any of us used the facilities, we made sure we returned the area back to how we found it. Additionally, each time we unpacked our bags and got dressed, we repacked our bags and placed them in a designated place in the room. We all made an intentional effort to keep the suite neat and orderly. Now, we never had a discussion about where we would place our bags after getting dressed or keeping the room clean, it was automatic. Additionally, when there was a suggestion of where to eat or hang out in the area, there was no long discussion or arguments. We simply made a decision and executed. Everyone was in sync. As I reflected on other past encounters, it dawned on me that we have always operated in this manner. Then I wondered if it was because of our *Pledge Process*. The conclusion that I came to was, yes it was.

So, whenever I hear about failed relationships or *Marriages*, I always wonder what type of "intentional preparation" took place prior to the failed *Marriage*. In many cases there was very little preparation outside of spending time together, meeting the in-laws, a few counseling sessions with a religious official, and asking a few surface questions that were pretty easy to answer. Do you think this is sufficient preparation for such an important decision? As far as pledging for a fraternal organization, you have to learn a lot about your line

mates, including but not limited to birthdates, names of all immediate family members, likes and dislikes, biggest fears, future goals, and many other aspects of a person's life. Along with spending an abundance of time together, a bond is created and can continuously grow, but only if you work as a unit.

My observation in Pontiac combined with numerous relationship conversations over time sparked an epiphany. My epiphany was, if couples implement some type of *Pledge Process* in their relationship prior to matrimony, maybe there will be more successful *Marriages*. In some cases, couples may even find out through the process that they shouldn't be together in the first place. It's no different than people aspiring to be a part of any institution, but through the initial process discover either they don't have what it takes to be a part of that particular organization or they simply lose interest and move in a different direction.

First and foremost, this process is for individuals that think they may want to pursue a long-term relationship. An optimal time to implement the *Pledge Process* is when you think the person you're dating might be "The One," and if you are unsuccessful, there is still time to back out. Don't wait until the engagement. It may be too late. Now, let's revisit your *Wish List*, as well as your potential life partner's *Wish List*. Before you get started, make sure your lists complement each other.

They don't necessarily have to match. However, you definitely want the list to have a connection. Once you verify compatibility, you can now move on to pre-planning and outlining your personalized marital *Pledge Process*.

Now, find a quiet place, just the two of you. Take paper and pen and each of you write a list of what you feel your personal deficiencies are. The more transparent, the better. Put those lists to the side. Now, write a list of deficiencies that you feel the other person needs to address. Be brutally honest, but fair. Then compare and compile a list as a unit and construct a plan to assist each other with making improvements. If executed properly, this exercise should yield optimal results, making for a stronger relationship. Make sure to maintain an open heart and mind throughout this portion of the process.

Before we get to the main details of the process, there is one more preliminary task. All organizations have laws, rules, commandments, and core values that they live by, which essentially represent their foundation. This foundation guides and governs their everyday movements. I recommend that you create a series of principles for the foundation of your potential union. Not only can these principles guide your relationship, they can also be a source of strength and inspiration during times of despair. Examples are trust, humility, monogamy, friendship, discernment, and spirituality. As a team create a list

of values that not only represent who you are, but also what you strive to become in the future. You may even want to create a special quote or affirmation that you will recite together on a daily basis. Let's see what the rest of this process may look like.

Your *Pledge Process*

You may or may not want to put a time limit on your process. I remember experiencing my *Pledge Process* and the individual that was assisting us with becoming members of the fraternity allowed us to have an open forum to ask any questions related to the process. Our main question was, "When will the process be over?" His reply was, "When you show ingenuity, teamwork, and allegiance as a group." As I reflect on that period, that is exactly when the process concluded and we became full-fledged members. So, you may want to concentrate more on the objectives versus time restraints. Now, create a check list for your *Pledge Process* together, but also determine the purpose for each item on the list. Review the sample check list below.

> ☑ *Spiritual, Mental, & Physical Health:* Set goals to improve your spiritual, mental, and physical health. These goals may consist of routine self-reflection, meditation, self-study of an array of subject matter, losing weight, reaching a certain body fat percentage, and fostering a healthy diet. Also, if

you hadn't already started, begin swimming, cycling, running, hiking, and maybe even yoga. You may also consider participating in a marathon, triathlon, or other related activities as a couple.

Purpose: Improving and maintaining your spiritual, mental, and physical health will set a precedent of healthy living for you individually and your family as a whole. It will also help minimize the chances of a spouse experiencing an untimely death, leaving the other to endure a *New Normal*.

☑ *Book Club:* Just like you have a book club with your girlfriends, form a book club with your future husband. Choose a list of books from different genres, fiction and non-fiction. Read and discuss the books together on a weekly or monthly basis.

Purpose: Reading and reflecting on various works of literature is a great way to spend quality time together. Additionally, you may learn about various aspects of how your significant other thinks and how they process information as it relates to various areas of life.

☑ *Travel:* Travel together, domestically and internationally. Experience different cultures for the first time together. Create memories you only have with that one special someone. Also, plan a road trip together, from the Atlantic to Pacific Ocean.

Purpose: When you travel with a person, you can learn a wealth of information about each other while experiencing a high level of self-discovery as one unit. As far as road trips, when you're in a car with someone for an extended amount of time, you have an array of conversations and you find out a lot about a person, some good and maybe some things that you were not necessarily expecting to discover.

☑ *Self-Discovery Outings:* Seek out and participate in activities that are "out of the box." These activities may consist of zip-lining, white water rafting, skydiving, scuba diving, hiking, camping, cave diving, and rock climbing, just to name a few.

Purpose: More times than not, activities that are considered "out of the box," are activities that are out of people's comfort zone. Therefore, there may be some trepidation. However, these types of experiences may help you conquer certain fears and discover various parts of you that you didn't know existed. These experiences will either bring you closer together or push you apart.

"God places the best things in life on the other side of maximum fear."
- Will Smith

☑ *Family:* Visit and spend quality time with various family members that are close as well as distant relatives on both sides. Also, ask questions about deceased relatives to learn family history.

Purpose: You may want to be familiar with not only the person you plan to marry, but also the people that are connected to that individual. Remember family genes, personalities, and ideologies are transferred in a multitude of modes from generation to generation. You may want to be familiar with the history of family members' health, mental and physical. Character traits and physical attributes may also be relevant. As a result of discovering family traits and family health issues that are adverse in your opinion, you may elect not to take a chance and marry into a family that may yield children with questionable character traits and health issues you don't want to be associated with.

☑ *Finances:* Have a detailed credit check completed for both parties. Agree to pay off all outstanding debt. This includes outstanding medical bills, credit card debt, and any other loans with the exception of student loans. Create a plan of how monies will be saved, invested, and allocated.

Purpose: Before you begin your new life with someone else, you may want to get your "financial house in order." You don't want to take financial problems into a new *Marriage*. Alleviate financial issues before they happen.

☑ *Cultural & Religious Exploration:* Explore different cultures, religions, rituals, and belief systems. This can be accomplished by visiting various Temples, Synagogues, Shrines, Churches, Mosques, and other Religious Centers. Additionally, meet and interact with people that look, speak, and think differently than you.

Purpose: Many individuals in the world follow a particular belief system or religion. These are the same individuals that you work with. These are the same individuals that will have children that will attend the same school your children will attend. Ultimately, when you leave your comfort zone and go out into the world, these are some of the people you will encounter. People are generally afraid of what they don't understand. Ignorance breeds fear, misunderstandings, and division. Learning about other people's belief systems, religions, and overall ways of life help build bridges of understanding. You don't have to agree with everything, just respect other people's right to live their lives how they choose. Ultimately, learning and becoming accepting of others helps to bring citizens of the world closer together. This concept can also be applicable to *Marriages*, bringing couples closer together.

☑ *Community Service:* Explore you're your inner humanitarian by helping others. Volunteer with local non-profit organizations to feed the homeless, pick up trash, mentor at-risk youth, or visit the elderly at a local senior citizen facility.

Purpose: Participating in community service projects together will not only help strengthen your community, it also promotes personal growth and self-esteem. Additionally, it will help foster a stronger relationship, because you are doing positive work together.

☑ *Something New:* Learn something new. This may include a new language, an instrument, board games (e.g., chess), cooking and dance classes, or participating in basic home repair workshops.

Purpose: These are extracurricular activities which couples can experience together. They are a change of pace from the typical dinner and a movie date. Hopefully, these types of activities will help couples prevent complacency and strengthen the relationship, overall.

Every process is different. The above-mentioned process or parts of the process may or may not be for you and your situation. That's fine. This list can be as expansive or as simplistic as you want it to be. Tailor your process to suit the needs, wants, and personality of your relationship. The most important thing is that you create the process together and make sure you see it through to the end, whether you decide to move forward or cut your losses and move in alternate directions. If you choose to move forward, along with completing a successful process, you may also want to continually discuss specific questions and discuss various topics that may have a direct impact on your relationship, presently and possibly in the future. Also, remember the real *Pledge Process* doesn't begin until after the wedding and honeymoon have concluded.

LEMONADE

BIG PICTURE

In pursuing a relationship, if your only objective is <u>Playing For The Ring</u>, you are playing yourself and the game is already over before it has begun. Being in a successful relationship is not a sprint, it's a marathon. Remember that nothing worth having comes easy. Everything that develops in life must go through a maturation process. Relationships are not exempt. Let your relationship develop effortlessly and organically, don't rush it. It takes preparation, sacrifice, fidelity, reciprocity, and that one intangible ingredient, chemistry, to cultivate a truly successful relationship.

"You can plan a pretty picnic, but you can't predict the weather."
- Andre Benjamin, Ms. Jackson

There is no one blueprint for a successful relationship. However, there are certain preemptive strategies you can apply

prior to entering a relationship that may prevent a series of lifelong heartaches. That means being more logical versus emotional. This strategy does not guarantee a successful *Marriage*; however, it may increase your chances of having a more successful relationship because logical decisions yield more optimal outcomes than emotional decisions.

> *"Remember in the game of life, some people play chess, others play checkers. If your main objective is acquiring a Ring, you're definitely playing checkers."*
> *- Imhotep Ja*

Playing For The Ring is not the Ma'at, Tora, Bible, or Qur'an. It's simply a compilation of research, my personal observations, experiences, and other people's situations that I've been privy to. You may not agree with all or any of this body of work. My challenge for you is to utilize your mental and spiritual filter to extrapolate the pertinent information that will enhance your life and disregard any information that is not useful. I don't profess to be an authority on relationships. Also, I don't claim to know everything about men and women and how they think. However, I've had enough experiences to know that relationships are a dichotomous paradox, simple yet complex.

BIG PICTURE

"In life, there are peaks and valleys. Never let your highs get too high and never let your lows get too low."
- Aki

We are living in a new age where the relationship rules of yesteryear don't necessarily appear to apply today. There may be a modicum of adjustments. The approaches you take and the measures you apply to a particular relationship are contingent on how well you know yourself and simultaneously recognizing the needs, wants, and expectations of yourself and others. Ultimately, you have to strategize not only how you're going to proceed as it relates to <u>Playing For The Ring</u>, but how you're going to connect with your best friend/soul mate to build a solid team where you are both constantly in lockstep, nurturing a lifelong union.

So again, <u>Playing For The Ring</u> is not the gospel or a binding authority for the success of all relationships. However, it is somewhat of a decalogue in that it is a playbook that assembles the rules of the relationship game, from my perspective. Additionally, it's a point of reference that can be applied in a proactive manner to minimize disastrous situations. It can also be utilized to address any classic situations as they arise in relationships, to prevent collateral damage, in real time.

Relationships between men and women have existed since the beginning of time and they will continue long after

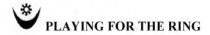

you and I are gone. The question is, when it's your move, how are you going to play it? Will you win or lose? Ultimately, it's your choice and remember, the game don't change, just the players and you are your only competition.

"Smart people learn from their mistakes; wise people learn from other people's mistakes."
- Wise Person

ACKNOWLEDGEMENTS

I would like to acknowledge all the individuals that contributed to the birth of <u>Playing For The Ring</u>. First, I would like to thank Stephanie Bowden for convincing me to create this body of work and hosting my first relationship forum. Prior to her influence, a relationship book was not part of my literary trajectory.

I would like to thank Keisha Wardlaw for retrieving my USB drive I left in the classroom where I had my interview for an adjunct professor position at Virginia College. This drive not only had the contents for the customer service demo class I presented, it also had the current and only draft for <u>Playing For The Ring</u>. She not only found the USB drive, she drove an hour from Columbia, S. C. to meet me in Augusta, GA to return the drive. If not for her, I would have had to start from scratch. I am forever grateful.

I would like to thank all the individuals that contributed their editing skills to various parts or the entire book. Starr Rayford, JeNeane Hamilton, Dr. Tanile Wells, Asia Jones, Julye Williams, and Akil Mason were an intricate part of this journey. They not only used their critical eye to find and correct errors in the literature, they also brought welcomed balance to the finished product. Additionally, I would like to thank Maryiah Felentae and Kofi Johnson for their artistic contributions toward creating two phenomenal book covers.

Finally, I would like to thank my parents, Bobby and Carolyn Rosemond. Thank you for showing me an example of a *Marriage* that has endured the good and challenging times over 45 years and also being extraordinary parents. I am who I am because of you.

REFERENCES

Alexander-Floyd, N. G., & Smien, E. M. (2006). Revisiting "What's in a Name?" Exploring the Contours of Africana Womanist Thought. *Frontiers: A Journal of Women Studies, 27*(1), 67-89.

Barash, D.P., & Lipton, J.E. (2001). *The Myth of Monogamy.* New York: W.H. Freeman and Company.

Cherry, A. L. (1994). *The Socializing Instincts: Individual, Family, and Social Bonds.* Conneticut: Praeger.

Gardner, S. (2015). Choice Theory: Gender Roles And Identity. *International Journal of Choice Theory and Reality Therapy, 35*(1), 1 – 4.

Greene, R. (1998). *The 48 Laws of Power.* New York: Viking Press.

Hartwell, L. P., Erchull, M. J., & Liss, M. (2014). Desire for Marriage and Children: A Comparison of Feminist and Non-Feminist Women. *Gender Issues, 31,* 102 – 122.

Hooks, B. (1989). *Talking Back: Thinking Femenist, Thinking Black.* Boston: South End Press.

Kretschmer, T. (1998). De Beers and Beyond: The History of the International Diamond Cartel. *Reuters.*

Lundberg, S., & Pollak, R. A. (2015). The Evolving Role of Marriage: 1950 – 2010. *The Future of Children, 25*(2), 29 – 50.

Murdock, G. P. (1967). Ethnographic Atlas: A Summary. *Ethnology, 6*(2), 109-236.

Newbury, C. W. (1989). *The Diamond Ring: Business, Politics, and Precious Stones in South Africa, 1867 – 1947.* Oxford: Claredon.

Rotberg, R. (2014). Did Cecil Rhodes Really Try to Control the World? *The Journal of Imperial and Commonwealth History 42*(3).

Walker, A. (1984). *In Search of Our Mothers' Gardens.* New York: Harcourt Brace Jovanovich.

Whiteman, L. (2013). Animal Attraction: The Many Forms of Monogamy in the Animal Kingdom. *National Science Foundation.* Retrieved from https://www.nsf.govdiscove ries/di sc_ summ.jsp?cntn_id=126932

Wickler, W. & Kacher, H. (1974). *The Sexual Code: The Social Behaviour of Animals and Men.* New York: Doubleday.

Williams, J. C., & Jovanovic, J. (2014). Third Wave Feminism and Emerging Adult Sexuality: Friends with Benefits Relationships. *Sexuality & Culture,* 157 – 171.

Zeitzen, M. K. (2008). *Polygamy: A Cross-Cultural Analysis.* Oxford: Berg.

Zoellner, T. (2006). *The Heartless Stone: A Journey Through the World of Diamonds, Deceit, and Desire.* St. Martins Press: New York.

About The Author

Dr. Abdalla Rashad Tau is an accomplished entrepreneur, educator, author, and philanthropist. <u>Playing for the Ring</u> is his third published book. The titles of his previous books are <u>Delinquent to Doctor</u> and <u>Embracing Toby</u>. Dr. Tau is committed to cultivating consciousness, scholarship, cultural awareness, healthy living, and independent thought in individuals in the United States and abroad, with an emphasis on positive exposure through various experiences. Dr. Tau believes education is a continuous process influenced by parental, school, and community factors, as well as self-discovery.

Dr. Tau is also an avid traveler, exploring more than 50 countries on seven continents and living in Tottori, Japan. The invaluable experience of working as an English as a Second Language teaching assistant in a Japanese rural village was the catalyst in establishing his non-profit youth organization, The Exposure Foundation. Dr. Tau understands that exposure to various levels of education, travel, positive encounters with people and experiences, and domestic/international travel has been the reason for a personal evolution from a juvenile delinquent to a doctor who mentors youth, which he discusses extensively in his inaugural book, Delinquent to Doctor. Dr. Tau believes that providing today's youth with inimitable opportunities will foster success and the encouragement needed to help young individuals avoid the many pitfalls life may present.

Among the many accomplished roles that Dr. Tau fulfills, being a life-long learner who believes in education versus indoctrination is his most cherished. He promotes teaching individuals how to think and look at life through a universal lens, creating citizens that will make positive contributions to a world society. His experiences and world travels have helped to develop a man consistently evolving with a desire to share and receive expertise and forethought with and from everyone he encounters. Dr. Tau further supports the community through affiliations with various mentoring programs, public/private schools, faith-based groups, and other non-profit organizations. Dr. Tau presently resides in Atlanta, GA.

Made in the USA
Columbia, SC
02 August 2017